Walk!
Costa del Sol
(Axarquía)

Nerja, Almuñécar, Cómpeta, Frigiliana
and the
White Villages of the Axarquía

with

Charles Davis

DISCOVERY WALKING GUIDES LTD

Walk! Costa del Sol (Axarquía)
ISBN 9781782750451

First Edition September 2017

Copyright © 2017

Published by
Discovery Walking Guides Ltd
10 Tennyson Close, Northampton NN5 7HJ, England

Maps are adapted from **Costa del Sol (Axarquía) Tour & Trail Super-Durable Map** published by **Discovery Walking Guides Ltd.**

Photographs*
Photographs in this book were provided by the author/researchers.

Front Cover Photographs

Árchez & La Maroma
(Walk 9)

The path to Los Pradillos (Walk 30)

Cerro Caleta (Walk 26)   Los Cahorros (Walk 23)

Text and photographs © Charles Davis 2017

Costa del Sol(Axarquía)
CONTENTS

'2 Walker' Itineraries

'3 Walker' Itineraries

'4 Walker' Itineraries

After twenty years travelling the world pretending to be a teacher, **Charles Davis** concluded that wandering about mountain tops was a more productive way of spending his time than standing in front of a classroom, a decision that has lead to over a dozen books for Discovery Walking Guides.

He is also the author of several novels, published by The Permanent Press. He is accompanied in his peregrinations by Jeannette (a refugee from the French education system) and assorted dogs that other people saw fit to dump in the local Rescue Centre, often for very good reasons.

For more information, see:-

http://charlesdavis2.wix.com/charlesdavis

ACKNOWLEDGEMENTS

As ever, for the without whoms: Jeannette, Ros, David, and the many pathmakers for whom walking was not always a pleasure.

Nerja, Almuñécar, Cómpeta, Frigiliana and the White Villages of the Axarquía

The Costa del Sol has often been mistaken for the epitome of all that is wrong with modern tourism, but in this publication we celebrate a Costa del Sol that does not correspond to the clichés, a Costa del Sol that is all right rather than all wrong, a playground of green valleys and gilded mountain tops, a hidden idyll unknown to most visitors, a haven for dedicated walkers and adventurous tourists alike, a place in which every nook is graced with some gratifying discovery and every outing is a great adventure.

The mountains of Nerja (Walk 30)

Covering the best preserved stretch of coastline, the prettiest villages, and most spectacular mountains, Walk! Costa del Sol explores the Axarquía region east of **Málaga**, an area blessed with grand summits, dizzying pinnacles, dramatic crags, deep ravines, delightful streams, stunning views, and the finest coves on the Costa del Sol, and all of it knitted together by a network of paths, trails, tracks and lanes so beguiling that walking is by far the best way to explore this lovely landscape.

.. beguiling lanes .. (Walk 19)

The Coast: Torre del Mar, Torrox Costa, Nerja, Maro, Almuñécar

The two main resorts in the west of our area, **Torre del Mar** and **Torrox**, are not the most picturesque, but they do have good climates (**Torrox** claim theirs is the best in Europe!) as well as a decent mix of accommodation options and a full range of services, so they are worth considering as a base.

Playa de las Doncellas (Walk 26)

Moreover, they are well-placed for accessing the itineraries between **Canillas de Aceituno** and **Cómpeta**. However, for a more photogenic coastal base, the resorts further east are preferable, notably the small town of **Nerja** and its satellite village, **Maro**.

Named for its abundant springs (Arabic *narixa*), **Nerja** is a peaceful place, and well preserved compared to the high rise resorts west of **Málaga**. The pedestrianised streets near the **Balcón de Europa** (a clifftop promenade named, according to local legend, after the rapturous exclamation of a nineteenth century king) are a pleasant spot for a stroll and the municipality is said to boast 16 kilometres of beach (I confess, I took this on trust and didn't measure them).

A centre for silk production during Moorish times, **Nerja** subsequently turned to other horticultural produce, notably sugarcane (the refinery and the aqueduct supplying it with water, the **Puente del Águila**, still stand on the outskirts of town) and latterly semi-tropical fruits, above all avocado. It is famous for the **Cuevas de Nerja**, a series of spectacular caverns with a cultural history stretching from Palaeolithic cave paintings to contemporary concerts.

Maro, just east of **Nerja**, is about as near as you'll get to an authentic Spanish village on the coast, its whitewashed buildings typifying the traditional vernacular architecture of the Mediterranean. If you want to be on the coast and prize peace and quiet over nightlife and shops, this may well be the place for you.

Maro and Cerro Gordo (Walk 12)

Beyond **Maro**, we have the **Acantilados de Maro y Cerro Gordo**, a rugged landscape of cliffs and coves classified a Natural Protected Area and featuring some of the best preserved coast to be found in Andalusia. At the eastern end of this area, our definition of the Costa del Sol becomes a little elastic, as we also annex a stretch of the Costa Tropical.

Named for its subtropical microclimate, the **Costa Tropical** exploits the copious waters draining off the **Sierra Nevada** to irrigate market gardens specializing in

Almuñécar (Walk 5)

tropical fruits. The most emblematic of these is the *chirimoyo*, one among many spellings for the fruits of the Soursop Family, better known in English as custard-apple, and lauded by Mark Twain as the most delicious fruit known to man. The taste is as protean as the name, having been

9

compared to strawberry, pineapple, papaya, peach and banana. For what it's worth, I'd suggest vanilla, but try it ripe from the tree and make up your own description!

Almuñécar, the main resort on the **Costa Tropical**, is a far cry from the sleepy fishing village Laurie Lee lived in prior to the Civil War, a period he describes in his memoir *As I Walked Out One Midsummer Morning,* where the town is glossed as 'Castillo' to protect the protagonists from Falangist reprisals. If holidaying there or in the smaller neighbouring resort of **La Herradura**, there are some classic walks starting from the **Carretera de la Cabra Montés**, the old road linking the coast with **Granada**.

The Mountains: the Sierras de Tejeda & Almijara

Though superficially coherent (their morphology is comparable, both are part of the Baetic Cordillera, and both have been incorporated into a single *Parque Natural*), the two sierras featured here are distinct.

The **Sierra Tejeda** (named for the abundant *tejos, taxus baccata,* a variety of shrubby yew) is a discrete massif defined by cliffs, gullies and gorges, and culminating in the Iberian Peninsula's westernmost 2000 metre summit (**La Maroma**, Walk 35), while the **Sierra Almijara** (probably from the Arabic *almijar* or 'draining

Lucerillo (Walk 36)

Walk 35, Sierra Tejeda

board', for the rapidity with which rainwater pours off the summits) comprises numerous mini-ranges aligned on a very approximate north-south axis and separated by a series of canyons. The traditional dividing point between the two sierras is **Puerto de Cómpeta**, which we visit in Walk 36.

The joys of these mountains are manifold, including bulbous karstic domes and vertiginous pinnacles, dramatic cliffs draped with ragged crags and grand ridges dominating the glittering blue sea; there are uplands patched with ancient pastures and dotted with the ruins of remote *cortijos* (farmhouses), there are terraces stippled with olive and almond trees, hillsides swaddled in a buttery blanket of yellow-flowering shrubs, valleys flanked by shady forests of conifer and cork oak, and fabulous ravines twisting between towering chicanes (known as *cahorros*) and tipping over spectacular waterfalls into deep plunge pools . . . and all of it accessible within fifteen minutes of the coast, which means we have the inestimable privilege of climbing a mountain in the morning and having a bathe in the Mediterranean in the afternoon.

The *Pueblos Blancos* of Andalusia with their whitewashed walls and red-tiled roofs are justly famous and the Axarquía does not disappoint in this respect. The best known *pueblos blancos* and the main gateway destinations for walkers are **Cómpeta** and **Frigiliana**. Both have expanded considerably in the last thirty years, but they've not lost their charm, and have survived as thriving communities in large measure thanks to the influx of foreigners.

Between the two lies **Acebuchal**, long known as the Lost Village or Village of Ghosts after its clearance in 1948 because the residents were suspected of supporting the Republican *maquis* who continued to resist Franco's regime, a battle detailed in local author David Beard's *Between Two Fires - Guerrilla war in the Spanish sierras*.

Acebuchal (Walk 3)

Canillas de Albaida (Walk 9)

But in the late nineties, the family of one of the dispossessed villagers returned and painstakingly rebuilt the village, opening a tavern and five *casas rurales*. Lost no more, **Acebuchal** has become a firm favourite with tourists, and is the place to stay if you really want to get away from it all.

West of **Cómpeta** are some of the region's prettiest villages, the two **Canillas** (**Aceituno** and **Albaida**), **Sedella**, **Salares** and **Árchez**. It's only comparatively recently that these *pueblos* have been taken up by foreigners, and they remain distinctively Spanish, albeit with evident Moorish origins in the fine *mudéjar* architecture.

Walk 19, views behind Sayalonga

All of these villages (and a few more besides) feature in Walk! Costa del Sol, either as destinations or the starting point for discrete walks.

The Walks

Spain is a place of paths par excellence, with a network of local ways linking villages, hamlets and farmsteads, while snow-gathering and transhumance trails climb the high peaks, and mining tracks penetrate the valleys. But perhaps the most important points of access are the old trading routes traversing the mountains, *caminos* that have left in their wake improbably remote ruined *ventas* (muleskinners' inns) and a long history of banditry.

Making best use of this rich walking heritage, we offer itineraries catering to a wide range of walking capacities, encompassing holidaymakers who just want to potter about within easy reach of the car and the outward bound enthusiast determined to scale the most obdurate summits. However, by far the greatest number of walks are aimed at the adventurous leisure walker, people who will on the whole have some experience of hiking in mountains, are happy to invest a certain amount of effort for a corresponding reward, but who do not measure pleasure by pain and potential danger.

In choosing itineraries, our guiding principals have been as follows:

On path (Walk 28)

1. Established itineraries on clear tracks and trails that won't be blocked by landowners
2. No off-path walking
3. Nothing too vertiginous
4. Avoid driving on dirt tracks to reach the start
5. Bus access where possible

Needless to say, like all rules, these are made to be broken and where the

Off path (Walk 11)

objective seemed sufficiently imperative, rules two, four and five have been broken, but in each instance, a warning is included in the itinerary introduction so you don't have any nasty surprises.

Dirt Tracks & Other Transgressions

Mountain walks in Spain often involve driving on dirt tracks to get to the start, yet most hire cars are not insured for off road driving. Moreover, rental agencies are increasingly alert to this issue and sometimes inspect the undercarriage of vehicles to make sure they haven't been off road, which is not necessarily a happy prospect when they have your credit card details! Some local companies do insure vehicles for off-road driving, so it's worth asking in advance if you can drive, for example, to the village of **Acebuchal** near **Frigiliana**, or to the **Pinarillo** *área recreativa* above **Nerja**.

Nonetheless, we have limited the number of walks that require dirt track access. We could have eliminated them altogether, but decided not to as this would have involved cutting some of the region's classic itineraries.

With the exception of Walk 13, all dirt track access walks cross reference alternative approaches on foot via other itineraries. If you do choose to drive on dirt tracks with a hire car, remember, <u>the vehicle may not be insured.</u> That's not necessarily a reason for not doing the walk. The tracks are drivable. But you are taking a risk. For other ways round this problem, see "Alternative Approaches" in the appendices.

As for breaking our other rules, the principal transgressions concern Rules Numbers Two and Five. Anyone familiar with mountain tops will know that rocky summits are rarely blessed with clear paths and the **Sierras de Tejeda** & **Almijara** are no exception.

Apart from Walks 11 & 23 (when you're paddling, the existence of a path or otherwise is a bit beside the point), the only itineraries that feature significant off-path sections are Walks 26 & 35. However, there are alternatives in each case, a stroll for Walk 26, and doing Walk 27 instead of Walk 35.

Cahorros (Walk 11)

Nearly every village featured in the book can be reached by bus, but timetables are often geared more to commuting and schooling than walking. When this is the case or a return trip would not allow enough time to do the walk, we don't mention the buses, but that doesn't mean you won't see a bus stop.

Timings

All timings are 'pure' excluding snacking, snapping and simply standing still staring, or what one Irish walker we met described as "putting it on while you're taking it off". All partial and global timings were taken from the 'Moving Time' recorded on the GPS. On big climbs, these are much shorter than actual progress. As a rule of thumb, the 'Stopping Time' on the GPS when I'm walking (that's just for breathers, discounting breaks) suggests you should add about 15 minutes in the hour.

If using GPS, you will soon see how your own moving time compares to mine. If not, do an easy route then multiply as required. For the strenuous walks, I have added an indication of the likely time you will need to complete the walk. All global data include the return except, of course, on one-way linear walks.

Hazards

The major risks one runs are the obvious ones of negligence or lack of foresight: dehydration when it's hot or disorientation when visibility is poor. Always take plenty of water, even when there's a *fuente* en route, and don't venture onto high ground in cloud or mist.

Processionary caterpillar nest

The only two natural hazards you are likely to encounter are processionary caterpillars (nose-to-tailing their way across a path or clustered in cottony nests in the trees), to which many people are allergic (take some antihistamine if you're susceptible to allergies), and brucellosis, an aggressive bacterial infection endemic among goats in Andalusia. The incidence of the disease is declining, but even so, if you cross a herd of goats, hold your breath.

When to go

Río Verde (Walk 13)

The walking season on the Costa del Sol is September to May. There are summer walks following riverbeds (i.e. **Río Verde**, Walk 13, **Río Chillar**, Walk 23, or the **Río Patamalara**, which we cross in Walk 8), but with highs hovering around 30 degrees, hill-walking can be uncomfortably hot.

Winters are mild and sunny, as the Atlantic fronts that bring rain to western Andalusia, and snow to the **Sierras de las Nieves** and **Nevad**a, tend to settle behind the coastal mountains. Bear in mind that seasonal terms are slightly different at this latitude.

'Winter' only really lasts for the two months of December and January, while 'Spring', to all intents and purposes, begins in February, when the first wild flowers bloom. For details of annual weather averages, see www.holiday-weather.com

Midwinter on Alto de Cielo (Walk 38)

On the whole, these are very forgiving mountains and most of the walks can be done with minimal equipment. I'd recommend good walking boots, but trainers or walking sandals are usually adequate and, indeed, essential when splashing knee deep up a river. Obviously, anyone inexperienced who climbs **La Maroma** in bad weather, or sets off without adequate sun protection or a supply of water on a hot day, is asking for trouble, but as a rule, if you don't ask for it, you won't get it, a quality of forbearance that is not always forthcoming in other ranges.

Facebook Page

To provide a resource for readers and walkers in the region, Walk! Costa del Sol has its own Facebook page, an open page on which anyone can post. Most welcome would be general feedback, photos, updates, and suggested alternatives. In the last instance, this could just be a few words, or a detailed walk description, or a link to your own walking blog, or simply to a file on a site like Wikiloc. Local businesses can post links, too, as long as they don't get too tedious! If there are daily postings about the absolute brilliance of Joe Bloggs' B&B, I'll delete them. In due course, updates will be collated in a single post to be pinned at the top of the page. Above all, though, I want to emphasize that this is a resource for you to use.

https://www.facebook.com/WalkCostadelSolAxarquia

Enough blather. Right now, there's another resource you've got to use: your legs. Let's get going.

Let's get going (Walk 1)

MAP PROVENANCE
Simplified and adapted map data provided by **Discovery Walking Guides Ltd.** (copyright David Brawn) has been used to prepare these location maps

The latest edition of Costa del Sol (Axarquia) Tour & Trail Super-Durable Map is available from booksellers. Digital mapping for this destination, and others, is available from:

www.dwgwalking.co.uk

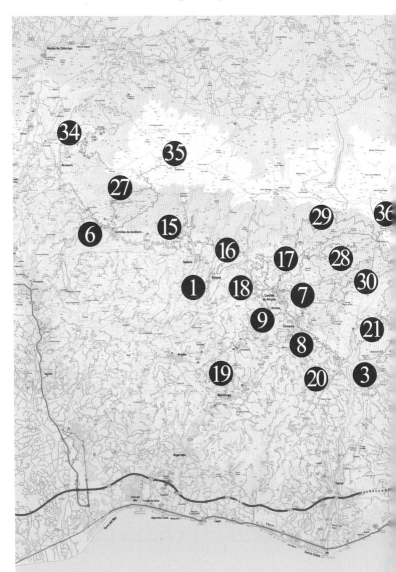

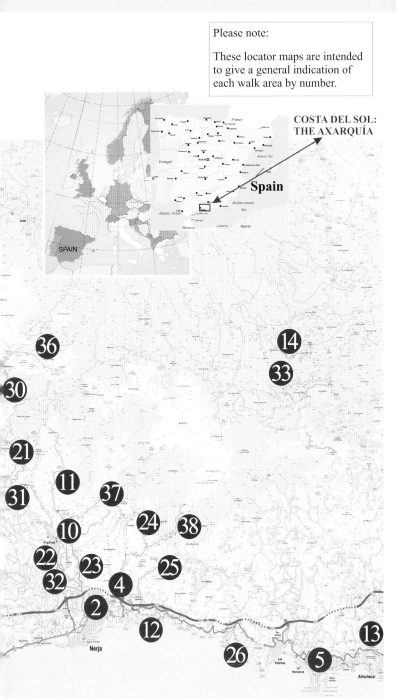

Please note:

These locator maps are intended to give a general indication of each walk area by number.

COSTA DEL SOL:
THE AXARQUÍA

Spain

DWG's Symbols Rating Bar shows key information about a walking route in a quick glance. Remember that effort/exertion and refreshment ratings are the authors' opinions and the time shown is walking time without stops.

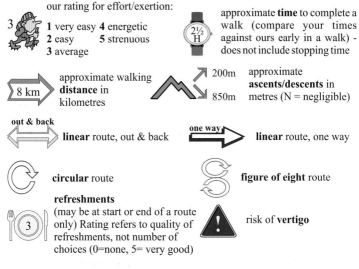

our rating for effort/exertion:

1 very easy **4** energetic
2 easy **5** strenuous
3 average

approximate **time** to complete a walk (compare your times against ours early in a walk) - does not include stopping time

approximate walking **distance** in kilometres

approximate **ascents/descents** in metres (N = negligible)

linear route, out & back

linear route, one way

circular route

figure of eight route

refreshments (may be at start or end of a route only) Rating refers to quality of refreshments, not number of choices (0=none, 5= very good)

risk of **vertigo**

Walk descriptions include: timing in minutes, shown as (40M), compass directions, shown as (NW), heights in metres, shown as (1355m) GPS waypoints, shown as (Wp.3).

A Note About Walking Times

Walking times create more discussion than any other aspect of walking guide books. Our walking times are for ***continuous walking*** at an easy pace without stops, representing the quickest time you are likely to complete a route. Most of us walk at a similar pace; approx 4-6kmh. As our routes are planned as fun adventures you are unlikely to simply march along the route from start to finish. We all take stops to enjoy the views, marvel at the flora, or simply to take a break. As a result, we suggest you add 25-50% to those continuous walking times, to allow for the stops you'll make along the route.

For particular details concerning the present publication, see page 13.

The map sections used in this book have been adapted from **Costa del Sol (Axarquía) Trail Super-Durable Map** (ISBN 9781782750390) published by Discovery Walking Guides Ltd.

Costa del Sol (Axarquía) Tour & Trail Super-Durable Map is a 1:40,000 full colour map. For more information on DWG publications, visit:

www.dwgwalking.co.uk

Altitude

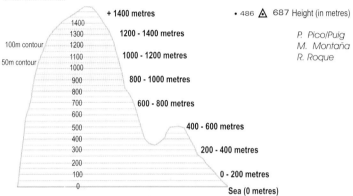

Roads, Tracks & Trails

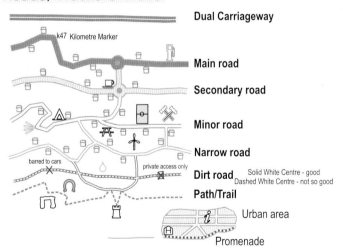

Walking Routes

19

Features

🠔 Mirador viewpoint   ◇ Spring   ⚒ Quarry   🎋 Picnic area   ⛽ Petrol

🍽 Cafe/Rest with   P Parking   𝑖 Information Office   ⚑ Sports Ground   ⊹ Cemetery

⛪ Church   ⛪ Chapel   ∩ Cave   🗼 Lighthouse   ♜ Tower   ⛺ Camping

🏨 Hotel   🏠 House/building   🏘 Large House   ⛺ Hut/Ruin   ✦ Wind Turbine/Windmill

USING GPS IN LA AXARQUIA

Every walking route in a Walk! guidebook can be easily and reliably navigated simply by following the detailed walk description. All of our routes are researched using a GPS so that we have an accurate record of where we have been. Even if you do not use a GPS yourself, you can be reassured that all Walk! routes have been accurately recorded.

Using a GPS with our waypoints will enable you to navigate the route with pin-point accuracy. Your GPS will show you where you are on the route in relation to the waypoints. Waypoints are provided for the key decision points on each walking route e.g. at trail junctions. Our GPS waypoints are most reassuring when you are adventuring in a new destination, as you know exactly where you are. Finding the start of a walk is simplicity itself as Waypoint 1 is at the start of each walking route.

GPS accuracy depends upon the local conditions affecting the reception of GPS signals.

Waypoint Lists for Costa del Sol (Axarquía) are available as a free download zip file, from www.dwgwalking.co.uk/gpxDownloads.htm; simply download the zip file and unzip it into its separate waypoint files in a choice of gpx, wpt or text waypoint files.

You can download the digital Costa del Sol (Axarquía) Tour & Trail Custom Map from DWG's website www.dwgwalking.co.uk The digital Custom map can then be viewed in Garmin Basecamp as a flat map sheet or in Google Earth where a transparent version is draped over Google Earth's 3D terrain model. You could also use the Custom Map as the basemap in your Garmin GPS. We are making all of our Tour & Trail maps available as free digital Custom Map editions so that you can view the map in full before deciding to buy the printed edition.

If you are interested to know more about GPS, we have made GPS The Easy Way available as a free download at www.dwgwalking.co.uk/gps.htm -

Remember:
A Compass points North
But a GPS shows you where you are,
Shows you where you have been,
And can show you where you want to go.

Following ancient cobbled trails and good dirt tracks with great views throughout, our first itinerary visits one of the Axarquía's best preserved and most beguiling villages, and serves as a good introduction to the Andalusian countryside. After crossing **Salares**' celebrated **Puente Romano**, we climb above groves of citrus trees, then traverse a hillside swathed in rosemary, beyond which the eponymous *monte* is terraced for cultivating almonds and olives.

The route is well wayposted and periodically waymarked. Once on trail, there is no need to consult the book.

Access: on foot from **Salares**. The village can be reached from the west via **Canillas de Aceituno** and the MA-4107, or from the coast via **Sayalonga** and **Cómpeta**, arriving via the MA-4108. Park in the main car park below **Meson Los Arcos** bar/restaurant at the southern end of the village.

Salares car park

The bridge at Wp.2

50 metres above **Meson Los Arcos**, we take the street climbing to the right into the heart of the old village, signposted with a ceramic plaque indicating (inter alia) 'Ayto / Consultorio / Iglesia / Puente'(Wp.1 0M).

Mapboards after the bridge

We then take the first turning on the left, a narrow alley which we follow until we see (down to our right), 'Calle del Puente', which leads to the bridge (Wp.2 3M), on the far side of which there are mapboards for the present itinerary and for Walk 16.

The path at Wp.3

Crossing the bridge, we follow a cobbled trail up to a waypposted junction below a 'Parque Natural' sign, where we double back to the right (Wp.3 6M) to climb along an intermittently balustraded path.

A brief but steady climb brings us up above the village, after which our path veers east and climbs more gently alongside a gully to a tall fingerpost (Wp.4 16M).

After briefly dipping down, we continue to climb amid tall clumps of broom, following a shaley trail heading toward the tail end of a rough track in an olive grove.

Near the end of the olive grove track, we bear left (Wp.5 22M), climbing steadily on a narrower path, skirting the upper reaches of the olive grove and heading for the highest of the three electricity pylons we can see above us. Beside the pylon, we join a dirt track (see photo on next page), which we use for most of the rest of the walk (Wp.6 25M).

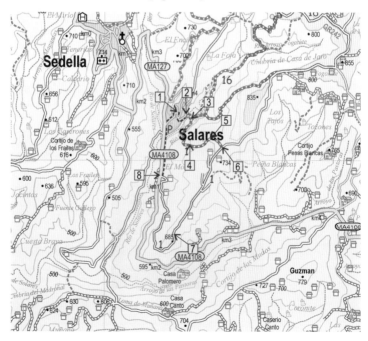

The ridge track

Turning right, we simply follow this track along the back of the ridge for the next 1200 metres, enjoying fabulous views and easy walking, and ignoring all branch tracks, notably toward the end of the ridge (Wp.7 40M), where a fork climbs to the right.

Staying on the main track, we contour round the hillside before descending amid olive and almond groves. A gentle stroll brings us down to the MA-4108 (Wp.8 60M), which we follow for 500 metres back to the start.

2 FRIGILIANA: NERJA via LOS CAHORROS

The second of our grade one walks links two of the Axarquía's top tourist destinations via the lower *cahorros* (the narrow stretches of a gorge) in the **Río Higuerón**. It's a wonderful outing that gives maximum adventure for minimum exertion.

The *cahorros*

The walking is easy, but it's worth noting that there are only patches of path in the bed of the river, the *cahorros* call for a ready tolerance of wild places, and unless you use the walkway (see text), you need to be ready for a bit of hands on bottom sliding descending the rocks.

As with all riverbed walking, do not venture down here after, during, or when heavy rain threatens. If you prefer to visit the *cahorros* on a circular route, see Walk 22.

ALT: start at Wp4

1 · 1H 40M · 7 km · 35m / 260m · one way · 4

Access: by bus
There is a regular bus service between **Nerja** and **Frigiliana**. **Nerja** bus station (Wp.8) is on the N340 at the NE end of town. In **Frigiliana**, stay on the bus until the main stop beside the playground in **Plaza Ingenio**. If arriving in **Frigiliana** by car, park along the bypass (*Circunvalacion*) or in the pay car park below **Plaza Ingenio**. In **Nerja**, there is a massive riverbed car park 200 metres south of Wp.7.

Our start at Wp.1

From **Frigiliana**'s **Plaza Ingenio**, we descend to the right of the 'Unicaja' bank on a concrete lane signposted 'Sendero', 'Río Higuerón' and 'GR249' (Wp.1). When the concrete bottoms out in the bed of the gorge (Wp.2 5M), we turn right, directly into the riverbed (see photo on the next page).

And that's really all you need to know, as we now simply follow the watercourse all the way to **Nerja**.

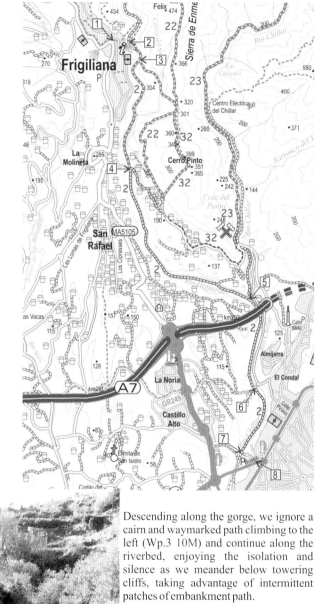

Descending along the gorge, we ignore a cairn and waymarked path climbing to the left (Wp.3 10M) and continue along the riverbed, enjoying the isolation and silence as we meander below towering cliffs, taking advantage of intermittent patches of embankment path.

After a little over a kilometre in the gorge, a stepped walkway appears on the left to help us through the *cahorros*; see the photo on the next page. You can take this straight away or continue slithering over rocks and under gigantic boulders of

The bed of the gorge (Wp.2)

The stepped walkway before Wp.4

agglomerate, just taking the steps toward the end, when we reach a drop sufficiently high to deter all but the most dedicated bottom-slitherer. 400 metres after the steps, the riverbed broadens and is crossed by a track (Wp.4 38M).

Carrying straight on, we follow a rough track along the riverbed, soon bringing into view the motorway viaduct, shortly before which we come to the confluence of the **Ríos Higuerón** and **Chillar** (Wp.5 62M).

Fording the **Chillar**, we turn right to pass under the viaduct, after which the track crosses a concrete road that is part of the **GR249** (Wp.6 82M). 800 metres later, 75 metres after a stretch of asphalting, we leave the riverbed, turning left beside an old factory (Wp.7 92M), and climb a concrete ramp into **Calle Joaquin Herrera**, at the end of which is the bus stop (Wp.8 95M).

The old factory at Wp.7

Cleared by the authorities in the late forties because its residents were suspected of sympathizing with Republican guerillas, **El Acebuchal** was for many years 'The Lost Village', derelict and largely deserted. It has now been found in a big way and is one of the Axarquía's must-dos.

El Acebuchal

This lovely little walk approaching the hamlet from the east follows the **GR249** along a dry riverbed, then returns via a dirt track with fine sea views and a tempting glimpse of **El Lucero** (Walk 36). A meal in the **Acebuchal** restaurant is required eating, though it would be a more natural stopping point on Walks 8 or 21.

1 · 1H 50M · 7.85 km · 160m / 160m · ↻ · 5

Access: by car
Follow **Frigiliana** bypass (*Circunvalacion*) to the 'Taller Los Cobos' roundabout and take the road out of the village setting the odometer at zero. Turn right for 'Acebuchal' at km2.5km on a narrow concrete lane.

Wp.1

The junction at Wp.2

Wp.1 is at the Y junction at the end of the concrete (km4.3), signposted 'Acebuchal 1.7km' and (to the left) 'Cortijo Ricardo'. There's a small concrete parking bay on the right. There's also parking 200 and 250 metres along the **Acebuchal** track, or at Wps.2 or 3.

From the end of the concrete (Wp.1 0M), we stroll along the **Acebuchal** track, following the **GR249**. 600 metres later, we fork left at a Y-junction (Wp.2 8M) and descend toward the hamlet. At the U-bend below the hamlet (the bar is

100 metres up to our left), we carry straight on along the GR (Wp.3 20M), climbing along the bed of the dry **Acebuchal** stream, signposted 'Puerto Verde'. Climbing gently amid pine and oleander, we follow the main streambed, ignoring all branches, all except one of which are shortcuts across meanders.

Wp.3

600 metres from the track, we pass below a limekiln, and continue climbing between increasingly impressive escarpments. When the GR climbs to the right on a wayposted path 550 metres after the limekiln (Wp.4 37M), we stay in the riverbed as it tunnels through the oleander until the next branch path, this time on the left (Wp.5 43M), which climbs to join a dirt track 50 metres later (Wp.6 44M). Turning right, we cross the streambed, briefly intersecting with the GR again. We follow this dirt track all the way back to Wp.2, climbing toward **El Fuerte** (Walk 31), and passing a rough track doubling back to the left (Wp.7 57M). At the foot of **El Fuerte**, the track begins to descend gently, passing an old quarry before rejoining our outward route at Wp.2 (101M).

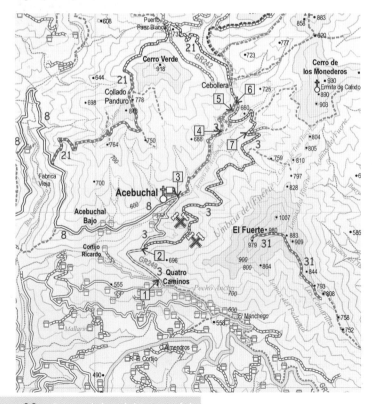

4

A classic combining minimal effort, magnificent isolation, and a ravine so addictive it ought to have deleterious consequences for your health, which it doesn't, so long as you don't descend into it during a deluge. Not to be missed.

Access: by car and bus
From exit 295 of the A7, follow the signs for 'Cuevas de Nerja'. Wp.1 is the 'Área Recreativa El Pinarillo / Fuente del Esparto' dirt track at the entrance gate to the *cuevas* car park. There is ample parking at the start of the track. There are regular buses from **Nerja** that stop inside the *cuevas* car park, 100 metres from the start. If you're staying in **Maro**, you'll find a footbridge to the *cuevas* crossing the motorway from the top of the village.

We set off along the 'Área Recreativa El Pinarillo/Fuente del Esparto' track (Wp.1 0M), following the **GR249** for 'Frigiliana'(Walk 37).

The track climbs gently then levels off as views open out over the lower reaches of the *barranco*.

Wp.1, our start point

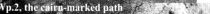

After 1.3km, we pass a rough track climbing to the right and a narrow path descending to the left. The path leads to the *barranco*, but for an easier descent, we carry on 50 metres to a cairn-marked path forking left (Wp.2 15M).

In the *barranco*

Wp.2, the cairn-marked path

Descending across bare rock and patches of path, we enter the *barranco* and another world altogether.

Turning right, we follow a shady trail along a dry watercourse (N) lined with pine, palm and eucalyptus and hemmed in by overhanging

29

cliffs of eroded agglomerate. The peace is absolute, despite the proximity of **Nerja** and the motorway. After a kilometre and a half in the ravine, we climb to the left briefly on a well beaten path bypassing a dry waterfall.

A little over 400 metres later, we bear right on a cairn and waymarked trail climbing onto the tail end of an old dirt track, now stripped of all its dirt and reduced to bare rock (Wp.3 43M).

Wp.3, the trail leading to the old dirt track

At the top of the old track, we rejoin the **GR249** on the main **Pinarillo** track (Wp.4 48M). Turning right, we follow the track back to the caves, passing the start of Walk 38, 200 metres after rejoining the GR.

Justly popular with holidaymakers staying in Almuñécar, the **Fishermen's Path** to the neighbouring resort of **La Herradura** is a lovely stroll, taking in a fine seafront promenade and the best preserved stretch of coast in **Almuñécar**. The title is no mere fancy as you probably will see fishermen plying the waters in front of the big hotels that have replaced more traditional pursuits as the mainstay of the local economy. There is a very, very slight risk of vertigo between Wps.4 & 5. The route is wayposted and intermittently waymarked.

Access: by bus
The official start is at **Cotobro** (Wp.2), which can be reached by the blue city bus Linea 1, but we recommend a more immediate start for those staying in **Almuñécar**, strolling along the promenade from the mouth of the **Río Seco** (Wp.1) next to the **Hotel Almuñécar Playa**, 150 metres west of the tourism office. If arriving in **Almuñécar** by car, follow the signs for the Tourism Office and park on the back streets behind the seafront. See below for ways back at the end of the walk.

Almuñécar promenade

From the bridge over the **Río Seco** (Wp.1 0M), we stroll along the promenade toward the west, passing the **Chinasol** apartment blocks, which make for a marked contrast with the cluster of upturned fishing boats on the beach. Continuing along **Paseo de Cotobro**, we pass the distinctive blue and white block of the **Hotel Arrayanes**.

The official start at Wp.2

The built up area ends as we round the headland to approach **Cotobro** and **Playa del Muerto**, above which we can see a small blue house, which we pass later. 300 metres after the **Hotel Playa Cotobro** bus stop, we reach the official start of the **Camino de los Pescadores** at the end of **Cotobro** seafront (Wp.2 32M).

31

Descending onto the beach, we take the tailored path below the cliffs at its western end.

Playa del Muerto

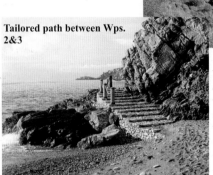

Tailored path between Wps. 2&3

We then cross the nudist beach of **Playa del Muerto**, towards the end of which, after a second stretch of tailored path, we take a wayposted path (Wp.3 39M) leading to concrete steps climbing a *barranco* behind the beach.

50 metres up the steps, we turn left as indicated by waymarks, onto a narrow path climbing across terraces, where we ignore a branch on the right (Wp.4 44M). Our path climbs steadily to steeply before skirting in front of the blue house, bringing the **Marina del Este** into view.

The wayposted path at Wp.3

Joining a dirt track behind the house (Wp.5 49M), we turn left toward our next objective, the ochre painted walls of the **Hotel Best Alcázar**.

The track, which narrows to a path toward the end, passes the **Mirador del Peñón Lobo** then emerges in front of the **Hotel Best Alcázar** (Wp.6 60M).

We carry straight on, passing to the right of an island of palm trees and bamboo, then descend on **Camino de la Playa**, the road into **La Herradura**. When the road doubles back to the left 100 metres later in front of **Casa Los Gemelos**, we cross onto a small circular *mirador* on the outside of the bend (Wp.7 64M).

Wp.7, at the *mirador*

Taking the steps below the *mirador*, we descend onto a track, the **Camino del Berenguel**, which is surfaced at this point. Turning right, we follow this track (which soon gives way to dirt before tarmac resumes for the final descent) all the way into **La Herradura**.

Passing in front of the **Edificio Montemar**, we have a choice. One option is to bear left to reach the seafront and sample one of the resort's many bars and restaurants before returning to **Almuñécar** by the blue city bus (Linea 2). The most easily locatable of the many blue bus stops is the one in front of the municipal market (*Mercado*) halfway along the seafront, at the eastern end of the large market building. There's no sign, but the stop is between the level crossing and the no parking sign.

Otherwise, to return directly to **Almuñécar**, cross the road in front of **Edificio Montemar** to pass in front of the church (Wp.8 73M). Carry straight on into the pedestrian zone of the old town and follow the main cobbled alley to the right. When the cobbling ends, we turn left and traverse the Dia Supermarket car park. Crossing the bridge in front of the supermarket, we follow the road up to the bus stop (Wp.9 80M) below the N340. The Linea 2 blue bus also stops here, but above all it is the ONLY stop for the more direct Alsa bus back to **Almuñécar**.

Brief but beautiful sums up this one as we follow a stretch of the **GR249** to a delightful hideaway, the **Cueva de la Fájara**, a potholer's paradise that tunnels into the mountain for over a kilometre and a half. The *nacimientos* are the source of the **Río Bermuza**, another beauty spot much prized by locals, especially in spring when the stream is in spate. The walk is easy, but you need to be sure footed for the descent after Wp.4 and bear in mind that the main climb is on the way back. The route is sign and wayposted.

Access: on foot from **Canillas**, which is best approached via the MA-4106 from **Vélez-Málaga**. If arriving by car, from the roundabout to the west of **Canillas**, take the road into the village and park on the right 400 metres later in the municipal car park. The bus service (from **Vélez-Málaga** and **Torre del Mar**) is limited, but adequate given the brevity of the walk.

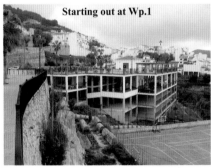

Starting out at Wp.1

From the car park (Wp.1 0M), we walk away from the village and past the bus stop back to the roundabout on the MA-4106. On the far side of the roundabout, we take the lane to the right of the **Vélez-Málaga** turning, as indicated by a GR signpost and mapboard (Wp.2 6M), and descend through olive groves, enjoying fine views over the western Axarquía.

After 700 metres of steady descent, we leave the lane at a sharp left hand bend, marked by GR wayposts and a large 'Cueva de la Fájara' sign (Wp.3 16M). Turning right on a narrow path, we descend across a partially interred *acequia*, before crossing a gully and traversing a spur, on top of which we pass a cairn marked branch doubling back to the right (Wp.4 19M).

Signboard at Wp.3

Long traverses zigzag down to cross one of the watercourses that form the **Río Bermuza**, after which we climb above the confluence of source streams.

Wp.5 seen from inside the cave

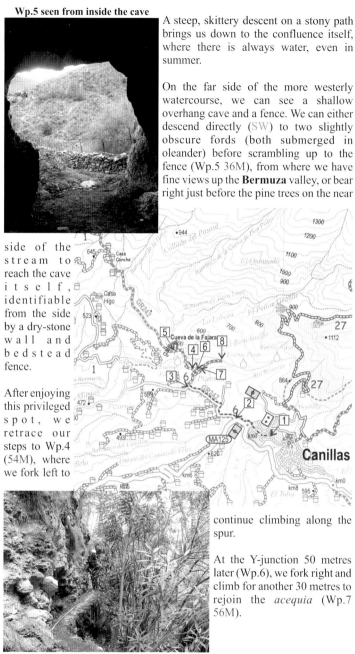

A steep, skittery descent on a stony path brings us down to the confluence itself, where there is always water, even in summer.

On the far side of the more westerly watercourse, we can see a shallow overhang cave and a fence. We can either descend directly (SW) to two slightly obscure fords (both submerged in oleander) before scrambling up to the fence (Wp.5 36M), from where we have fine views up the **Bermuza** valley, or bear right just before the pine trees on the near side of the stream to reach the cave itself, identifiable from the side by a dry-stone wall and bedstead fence.

After enjoying this privileged spot, we retrace our steps to Wp.4 (54M), where we fork left to

Approaching Wp.8

continue climbing along the spur.

At the Y-junction 50 metres later (Wp.6), we fork right and climb for another 30 metres to rejoin the *acequia* (Wp.7 56M).

Turning left, we stroll along the *acequia* for 300 metres to its source at the **Nacimientos** (Wp.8 61M). From here we simply retrace our steps and follow the *acequia* past Wp.7 until we recover our outward route.

35

A good introductory walk for getting the lay of the land. Following broad paths, tranquil lanes and good dirt tracks, the walking is easy and we enjoy good views throughout. There are no walk specific waymarks, but much of the itinerary follows the **GR249**, and nearly all the rest is on a single dirt track.

Access: on foot from Cómpeta

If arriving by bus (from **Algarrobo** and **Torre del Mar**), from the tourism office bus stop, take the road climbing to the left of the tourism office into **Plaza de la Axarquía**. Carry straight on past the 'Cajamar' bank then climb past the 'Eroski' supermarket on **Calle Rampa** to reach the church square (Wp.1). If arriving by car, drive to the car park in **Plaza de la Axarquía** and walk to the church square, as described for the bus access.

Starting out in the church square (Wp.1)

From the top of the church square (Wp.1 0M), we take the alley to the left, signposted 'Consultorio Médico' and 'Biblioteca Municipal', passing in front of **Bazar Andaluzi** gift shop. Carrying straight on at each junction, we pass **Hotel Balcón de Cómpeta** and **Ermita San Antonio**.

Wp.2, Ermita de San Antonio

Behind the *ermita*, we follow the road round to the right (signposted 'Avenida Canillas/Plaza del Carmen') for 25 metres to reach the sandy, balustraded balcony path of the **GR249** (Wp.2 7M).

Ignoring a fork on the left 75 metres later, we follow the GR, bringing into view **Canillas de Albaida** (Walk 9) and the region's highest mountain, **La Maroma** (Walk 35). The path runs parallel to the *acequia* that gives the route its name, then joins a backroad above **Canillas** (Wp.3 20M).

We carry straight on, toward the looming mass of **La Maroma**, bringing into view up to our right an electricity substation that serves as a waypost for our return route.

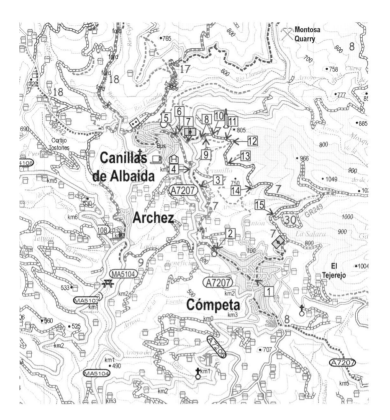

250 metres later we leave the road, forking left on a path as indicated by a yellow arrow painted on the road and a GR X-post directly ahead of us (Wp.4 23M).

Following a broad terrace path above the interred *acequia*, we traverse avocado orchards and olive groves. The path eventually runs into a track in the upper reaches of **Canillas** (Wp.5 29M).

We follow the track round to the right, ignoring yellow waymarks indicating a turning on the left 50 metres later.

When the track joins a road 75 metres further on (Wp.6 32M), we leave the GR, and turn right to climb past the village water plant and playing fields.

At the the end of the road, a slip path climbs to rejoin the road we left at Wp.4 (Wp.7 35M). Turning left, we climb along the road for 100 metres to the first left-hand bend, where a cairn marks a rough path off to the right climbing alongside olive groves (Wp.8 37M).

In the unlikely event of this path falling into disuse, continue on the road to the start of the dirt track below the electricity substation spotted earlier. Otherwise, follow the path alongside the olive grove, above which we reach a Y-junction (Wp.9 39M). We can take either branch, the one on the left joining the track a little earlier (Wp.10 42M), the one on the right a couple of hundred metres further east (Wp.11).

We now simply follow this track nearly all the way back to **Cómpeta**, enjoying fine views over **Corumbuela** and **Sayalonga** (Walk 19) and down toward the sea. 75 metres after the second path joins the track, we ignore a broad trail descending to the right (Wp.12 45M). After a gentle climb, we pass another broad trail, this time one that climbs to the left (Wp.13 49M). We then pass a rough branch track on the right (Wp.14 57M).

After three kilometres on the track, we rejoin the GR on the bend of another track (Wp.15 70M). Walk 30 climbs to the left here, but we bear right and follow the GR down to the far side of **Cómpeta** football field, where we turn right on a spur track (Wp.16 76M) leading to a rough path descending to the stadium access road.

Following the road down from the football ground, we descend directly into **Cómpeta**'s **Plaza del Carmen**, where we turn left, then descend to the right on a concrete alley. Descending at each junction, we reach a T-junction in front of house Nº60, where we turn left into **Rincón de los Abuelos** (Grandad's Nook). Turning right, we keep descending then take **Calle Dr. Fleming** into the church square.

8

Cited as the most popular itinerary offered by one local walking company, this walk visits the once 'lost' village of **El Acebuchal** (see Walk 3) from the west. Despite its length, it's very easy, all on dirt track and surfaced road, indeed the toughest bit is the first 500 metres climbing out of **Cómpeta** - always discounting the heroic effort required to prise yourself from your chair after a good feed at **Bar El Acebuchal**.

I referred to a meal here as 'required eating' in Walk 3 and the current itinerary is probably the one best calculated for indulging yourself at the restaurant. They're open from 10 to 5 every day throughout the year, but call first to be sure (661 514 834). Boots or sandals are better than shoes for the **Río Patamalara** ford.

Access: on foot from Cómpeta
The walk starts from the tourism office bus stop in **Cómpeta**, which can be reached by bus from **Algarrobo** and **Torre del Mar**.

If arriving by car, skip the first bit of the itinerary and start from Wp.7, km7.6 of the A-7207, a sharp left hand bend (approached from the south) with a dirt track on the right signposted 'Acebuchal', 'Zona Recreativa Fábrica de la Luz' and 'La Ruta del Acebuchal'. Park on the broad dirt platform at the start of the **Acebuchal** track. From here the return time is 2h40 for a distance of 13km.

From the **Cómpeta** tourism office bus stop (Wp.1 0M), we take **Calle Pilar**, 50 metres to the south, beside the 'Salamandra' sports shop.

At the junction with **Calle Mirador** 100 metres later, we take the lane on the right in front of house Nº39. Climbing at each junction, we emerge on **Avenida de Torrox**, where we continue climbing to the right to reach a railed slip path up to the left, joining the **Torrox** road (the A-7207) at the **Venta de Palma** intersection, just short of km4 (Wp.2 7M).

Forking left at Wp.3

Bearing left, we follow the A-7207 for just over a kilometre to a sharp right hand bend immediately after **Villa Kristina**, where we fork left on a track signposted 'Carril Zaja' (Wp.3 19M).

The track, which serves villa owners and goatherds alike, runs parallel to the main road. In front of the **Casa del Zorro** and **Casa del Ari** (Wp.4 29M), we bear right to pass below the two villas on a stretch that is the preserve of pedestrians. 400 metres later, we join another villa access track climbing from the road (Wp.5 33M). Carrying straight on, we follow this track until it ends in an eroded slope impassable to vehicles, where we descend alongside a partially exposed pipe to join a third track beside a red roofed bungalow (Wp.6 38M).

Turning right, we descend to the starting point for motorists, the **Acebuchal** track beside a yellow concrete hut (Wp.7 43M), where we turn left.

The **Acebuchal** track passes below a *cortijo* fronted by well-maintained grape drying beds. We follow this track all the way to **Acebuchal**.

The start for drivers (Wp.7)

Grape drying beds after Wp.7

There's only one turning en route, obvious and clearly signposted, so textphobes can stow the book now.

We soon see the summits of the **Loma de la Mata** and **Cerro Verde** (Walk 21) and **El Fuerte** (Walk 31).

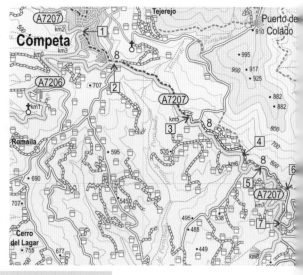

Descending into the Patalamara Valley

The track rapidly leaves behind the last of the housing and curls into the **Patamalara** valley, fabulous views opening out up towards **Lucero** (Walk 36).

Descending gently past a shrine and a small house, we ford the **Río Patamalara**, a

popular spot for river splashing fun in the summer.

A little over 100 metres later, our track doubles back to the right at a junction (Wp.8 70M), though if you fancy a break, it's worth carrying straight on for 50 metres to the old **Fábrica de la Luz área recreativa**.

Patamalara river ford

Returning to the **Acebuchal** track, we climb gently (S) for 1200 metes to a pronounced left hand bend where the track briefly levels off (Wp.9 90M), at which point we pass Wp.3 of Walk 21, a narrow path flanked by two cairns doubling back to the left. For the present itinerary, we continue along the track, soon climbing gently again before curving round to the east, bringing **El Fuerte** back into view.

A brief descent brings us down to **Acebuchal Bajo** from where a last gentle climb leads to the main hamlet and the highly recommended **Bar El Acebuchal** (Wp.10 116M). The wild boar is excellent and the vegetarian platter is sufficient to make meat eaters jealous.

We return (chair challenge notwithstanding) the same way.

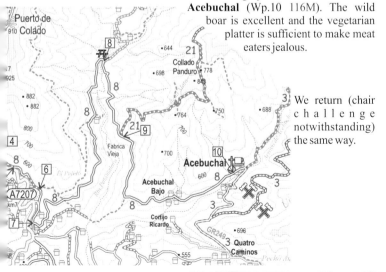

9 THREE VILLAGES: CÓMPETA, CANILLAS DE ALBAIDA, ÁRCHEZ

The local authorities call this '**The Wine Route**', which is a polite way of saying that it's something of a pub crawl. Visiting three villages, each boasting excellent hostelries, this is not a walk for anyone wanting to count the calories. Nor do I recommend it if you're hankering after grand vistas and dramatic mountains. But if you appreciate pleasant countryside, pretty villages, friendly locals, and a good 'pub crawl', let's go!

Of the many refreshment opportunities en route, we visited the **Avenida** in **Árchez** and the **Cerezo** in **Canillas**. If you're taking the pub crawl seriously, there are also two vineyards, **Bodega Lopéz Martín** in **Árchez** and **Bodega Jarel** below **Cómpeta**, the latter of which furnished the King of Spain with a few tipples for his nuptials.

The walk starts from **Cómpeta**, but it's worth considering starting in **Canillas**, doing the climbing early on and ending at the highly recommended **Bar Restaurant Cerezo**. If you take this option and don't want to visit **Cómpeta**, there's an alternative route to **Canillas** from Wp.20. If you don't like the sound of the barking dogs at Wp.12, turn left at Wp.7 then take **Avenida de Andalucía** down to the **Árchez** road and follow that to rejoin the described itinerary at Wp.14.

Access: on foot from any of the villages.
If starting from **Cómpeta**, see Walk 7 for access details. If arriving in **Canillas** by bus, from the bus stop in front of the tourism office, descend **Avenida Andalucía** into **Calle Estación**, joining the walk in front of the **Bar Restaurant Cerezo** (Wp.7). Car drivers can park in front of the tourism office. There's no bus service to **Árchez**, but plenty of room to park alongside the river (Wps.13&14).

The GR out of Canillas

The start from **Cómpeta** is the same as Walk 7 Wps.1-5. The relevant waypoints are included in the waypoint file for the present itinerary. Fifty metres after the GR joins the dirt track (Wp.5), we leave both track and GR, turning left, as indicated by a large yellow arrow on the concrete base of an electricity pylon up to our right (Wp.6 30M).

Descending a stairway between two houses, we recover the *acequia* path, which ends at a road on the edge of **Canillas**. Crossing the road, we carry

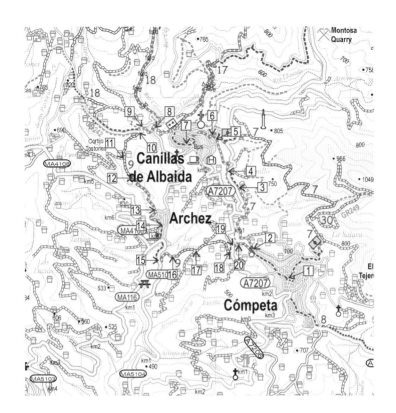

straight on along a concrete and brick lane (**Calle Carnero**, unnamed at the start).

When **Calle Carnero** narrows to an alley, we take **Calle San Antonio**, then turn right into **Calle Granada** and left 25 metres later in front of house Nº12. Descending at each junction, we join **Calle Estación** next to the **Bar/Restaurante Cerezo** (Wp.7 37M), where we turn right. We stay on **Calle Estación** for 250 metres until we see the brick archway of the cemetery gates ahead of us. Turning left (signposted 'Ruta Turistica al Pie, Paraje Natural, Fuente Santa, Rio Llana') then immediately left again, we rejoin the GR, which descends steeply onto a cobbled mule trail that zigzags down to a minor road. 25 metres down the road, we turn left (Wp.8 53M), still following the GR as it crosses the ancient **Puente Romano**.

After zigzagging up to rejoin the road, we bear left (Wp.9 58M), following the road round a bend, beyond which we leave both road and GR, turning left on a track signposted 'Lisa Katrina' (Wp.10 59M). Ignoring the branch on the left 30 metres later, we carry straight on to the right of house Nº4.

After passing between two villas, we turn left at a T-junction (Wp.11 65M) and descend past two more houses, the second of which is home to several noisy and not manifestly friendly dogs. The dogs' owners are friendly, but if you're nervous about dogs, this stretch can be avoided by taking the road between **Canillas** and **Árchez**.

43

The track ends at 'Rowdy Dog House' (Wp.12 68M), beyond which a rough path descends steeply across cultivated terraces to the **Río Turvilla**.

Heading downstream (SE), we ford the river four times before passing the picturesque **Molino Winkler** (AKA **Molino Dña Fidela**) and crossing a footbridge to reach the riverside promenade in **Árchez** (Wp.13 78M).

Árchez & La Maroma

We can either continue along the riverside, passing **Bar La Peña Cataollas** before climbing to the main road at the southern entrance to the village (Wp.14 83M), just past **Bar Avenida**, or reach the same point by traversing the village via **Puerta del Río**. The lively **Bar Avenida** is a good place to soak up the local atmosphere and contemplate the distant dome of **La Maroma** (Walk 35).

After Wp.14, there is a tricky pathfinding moment. We follow the road to the south, passing in front of **Bodega Lopéz Martín** and above the **Corumbuela** bridge. 600 metres south of the village, we pass a small house on our right with a distinctive lozenged metal gate. In the bend on the left there is a concrete ramp.

Wp.15

Just before the ramp, a fingerpost ('Árchez') and mapboard of local paths mark the point where a rough way climbs to a *cortijo* (fronted with pine, agave and a few sickly prickly pear bushes) just above the road (Wp.15 93M).

We take the rough path beside the signpost, then climb to the left of the *cortijo*, flush with its walls, ignoring the more obvious branch heading back towards the village.

Climbing steadily, we follow the path through an eroded chicane, after which it broadens to a trail leading to a dirt track (Wp.16 100M). We continue climbing steadily (ignoring minor branches accessing terraces) to a crossroads between a white reservoir and a cluster of *cortijos* (Wp.17 106M).

Turning left, we climb on an easier gradient, sticking to the main track until it joins the **Canillas-Cómpeta** road beside **Bodega Jarel** (Wp.18 113M).

Turning left, we follow the road for 75 metres then, immediately before it passes between two short crash barriers, turn right (Wp.19) on a narrow path climbing alongside a watercourse, at the head of which we join the remains of an old mule trail (Wp.20 118M). If you're not visiting **Cómpeta**, turn left here to follow the trail and its continuation as a path back down to the road, then walk along the road for a little over a kilometre to **Canillas**.

Otherwise, we turn right. If you started from **Cómpeta**, we rejoin our outward route 200 metres later behind the **Ermita San Antonio**. If you started lower down, at the top of the mule trail, carry straight on past the **Hotel Balcón de Cómpeta**, then fork left at the junction with **Calle Constitución** passing the *Biblioteca Municipal*, and carry straight on at every junction till you emerge at the top of the church square, where there are enough restaurants and *tapas* bars to satisfy anyone.

10 FRIGILIANA: BARRANCO DEL AGUJERO

An excellent first walk for getting a feel for the terrain around **Frigiliana** as it touches on all but one of the itineraries starting from the village. It also happens to be a very lovely walk in its own right, a perfect remedy for anyone suffering from a surfeit of noise, the only sounds likely to accompany us on our excursion being the soughing of wind in the trees, the scurrying of scuffling squirrels, the chirrup of birdsong, and the chuckle of running water.

Despite being an official **Frigiliana** itinerary and well-known to local walkers, the route rarely appears on maps. It's easy walking, the stiff climb back into **Frigiliana** at the end notwithstanding. Not recommended after, during, or when there is a threat of heavy rain.

Access: by car and bus from **Nerja**. If you're driving, park on the bypass (*Circunvalacion*) or in the pay car park below **Frigiliana**'s central **Plaza Ingenio**. If arriving by bus, stay on the bus until the main stop beside the playground in **Plaza Ingenio** (Wp.1).

Starting out at Wp.1

From **Frigiliana**'s **Plaza Ingenio**, we descend to the right of the 'Unicaja' bank on a concrete lane signposted 'Sendero', 'Río Higuerón' and 'GR249' (Wp.1 0M).

When the concrete bottoms out in the bed of the gorge (Wp.2 5M) (where Walks 2 & 22 descend to the right), we

carry straight on, upstream, on the dirt track for 'Sendero Frigiliana - Fuente del Esparto', still following the **GR249**.

700 metres later, we pass the **Pozo Batán** reservoir which used to double as a swimming pool, but is now sadly fenced off.

Wp.2, in the bed of the gorge

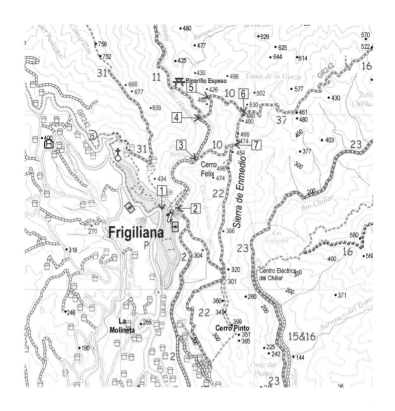

75 metres after the reservoir, the GR (and Walk 37) climb to the right (Wp.3 17M). We use this path for our return route, but for the present, we continue up the **Río Higuerón** (Walk 11).

The track runs alongside an *acequia*, then dips back into the riverbed at the terminus of an electricity line, 100 metres after which, we leave the **Higuerón**, turning right beside a twin-trunked pine on a narrow path marked by a large cairn and black waymarks (Wp.4 25M).

Turning right at Wp.4

The path climbs in easy stages then levels off before entering the bed of the **Barranco del Agujero**, the 'Ravine of the Hole' or 'Drain', a neat echo of the etymology of the **Sierra de Almijara** or 'draining board'. After a little over 500 metres of gentle climbing, the *barranco* widens and two large cairns indicate a clear path branching off to the right (Wp.5 37M).

The gradient steepens on the path, though never enough to get us gasping, as a steady, serpentine climb redolent of pine and rosemary brings us onto a spur, where superb views open out down towards the sea.

After climbing along the back of the spur, our path veers south to rejoin the GR (Wp.6 49M).

Approaching Wp.6

Walk 37 continues to the left here, but for our brief introduction to the area's potential, we turn right and follow the GR back to **Frigiliana**. 400 metres after rejoining the GR, the trail reaches a rocky pass on the back of the **Sierra de Enmedio** ('in the middle' because it divides the **Higuerón** and **Chillar** rivers) (Wp.7 56M), where Walk 22 feeds in from the left.

The two itineraries share the same descent as we simply carry straight on, following the GR as it zigzags down to rejoin our outward route at Wp.3 (1h12m).

11

Like most adults, I generally take 'infantile' to be a pejorative adjective, but when it comes to messing about in rivers, I'm all for a rapid regression to childhood. If you suffer a lurking urge to splash your way through that puddle or have fond memories of paddling in streams during your nonage, this is the outing for you, following the largely pathless course of the **Río Higuerón**, which is named for the fig tree said to grow at its source.

Until Wp.6 the walking is easy. Thereafter, the route becomes increasingly rough and the end is only recommended for the most agile, as an amusing time hopping from stone to stone becomes a hell-or-high-water scramble (a dunking is virtually guaranteed) up the chutes, waterslides and cascades of the *cahorros*, the straits toward the head of the river. Walking sandals or trainers are preferable after Wp.6 and essential after Wp.8. Do not venture into the ravine after, during, or when there is a threat of heavy rain.

*4, if you continue up the cahorros. See text.

Access: see Walk 10

Starting at Wp.1 (see Walk 10)

The start of the itinerary is the same as Walk 10 Wps.1-4, except that at Wp.4 we stay in the riverbed rather than turning right. The relevant waypoints are included in the waypoint file for the present itinerary.

And that's all you need to know until Wp.6, as we simply follow the course of the river, making use of intermittent stretches of track and path, but on the whole, hopping from side to side of the watercourse, winding between walls of oleander, esparto grass and reeds.

The recreation area at Wp.5

A little over 500 metres after Wp.4, we pass the **Pinarillo Espeso Área Recreativa** (Wp.5 31M).

Half an hour later, **Lucero** (Walk 36) come into view (see photo on page 51) and the valley widens, passing two dry affluents descending from the west.

49

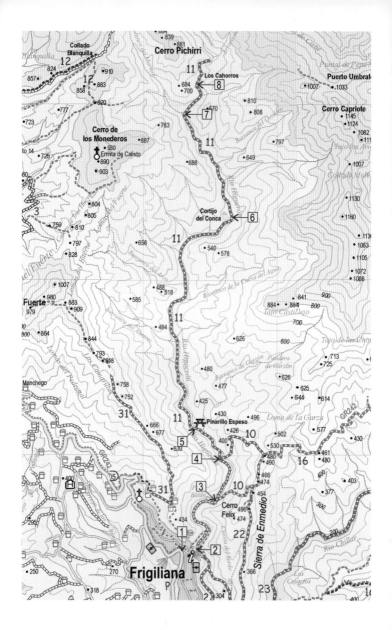

Below the ruins of **Cortijo del Conca** (camouflaged by the surrounding rocks), the river narrows between low cliffs then curves left toward the head of the **Acequia de Lisar** and a first waterhut (Wp.6 81M).

Most people will be happy to turn back here, but if you care to elevate the drama, you can continue to Wp.7 and, if you really want to go wild, carry on (I use the term advisedly) up the *cahorros*.

Lucero comes into view

In either case, it's time to put on your soakable footwear. Subsequent timings are very subjective, depending on the level of water and your own agility. After Wp.8, GPS reception is poor, but you won't have any hands free for consulting a GPS device - or a book for that matter.

The river becomes steeper and rougher as we approach a second, smaller waterhut, 75 metres after which we reach a first narrow stretch.

500 metres after the mini-straits, we come to the confluence of the **Río Higuerón** and the **Barranco del Marmol** (Wp.7 127M). If you continue, expect to get wet.

Bearing right, we follow the **Higuerón** toward the southern face of **Cerro del Cisne**, climbing more steadily, passing some fine jacuzzis.

Preparing for a dunking

400 metres after Wp.7, we ignore a faint way climbing to the left and instead continue upstream (Wp.8 142M), entering the extraordinary *cahorros*, clambering over six small and not so small waterfalls. Don't worry if you lose count, you'll know when you can go no further. Bear in mind that what's tricky on the way up is trickier on the way down.

Waterfall 7 - STOP!

Waterfall 1 can be skirted by slippery rocks on the right.
Waterfall 2 is awkward, especially if you don't have a very long reach.
Waterfall 3, immediately after No.2, is a doddle.
Waterfall 4 is high but dry (on the left) and has piled stones to help the climb.
Waterfall 5 is passed by a very rough way over the rocks on the left.
Waterfall 6 is torrential, but using a boulder on the left, still passable.
Waterfall 7 (162M) Stop!

We return by the same route
... slowly.

The Martello towers dotted along the Costa del Sol betray an uneasy history of clashing cultures and good old-fashioned piracy. In this short itinerary, we visit one of the best preserved of these towers and enjoy fine views over the equally well preserved **Acantilados de Maro y Cerro Gordo** coastline.

Access:

On foot from **Maro**. If arriving by car, the car park (Wp.2) below **Plaza Iglesia** can be reached from the roundabout on the N340 at the eastern end of **Maro**, signposted 'Parking Maro', 'Playa Cala de Maro'. If arriving by bus, from the roundabout bus stop at the western end of the village, follow the road into **Maro** then turn right into **Calle Real**. **Plaza Iglesia** is at the end of **Calle Real**.

The *plaza* at Wp.1

From the southern end of **Plaza Iglesia** (Wp.1 0M), we take the brick stairway descending between the car park and the ruins of the **Ingeniero** sugar works onto the beach road below the car park (Wp.2 1M).

Bearing right, we follow the road for 700 metres, descending past the village's densely packed hothouses, until it doubles back to the right above the beach.

Immediately after the U-bend, we fork left on a roughly metalled track (Wp.3 11M). After climbing for 200 metres, the track swings sharp left below a hothouse, at which point we bear right (Wp.4 15M) on a minor branch that immediately dwindles to a narrow path.

Bearing right at Wp.4

After passing below the hothouse, the path joins the end of a dirt track. We follow the track across an avocado plantation and up to a crossroads below pine trees and a 'Paraje Natural' signboard (Wp.5 23M).

Carrying straight on, we continue climbing to an inverted Y-junction (Wp.6 26M), where we double back to the right.

Forking left at Wp.7

The track descends gently to a broad platform, 10 metres beyond which, we fork left on a path (Wp.7 30M). Ignoring a minor branch on the right 40 metres later, we climb steeply on log steps to reach the *torre* (Wp.8 33M).

The *torre* (Wp.8)

Heading inland on the broad trail behind the *torre*, we pass a limekiln 300 metres later (to our left and invisible from the path, but marked by a couple of cairns) and a branch path doubling back to the right 200 metres after that (Wp.9 43M).

We then cross a small rise and descend to a path behind the crash barriers on the N340 (Wp.10 47M). We follow the roadside path back to the village.

13 ALMUÑÉCAR (Carretera de la Cabra Montés): RÍO VERDE via FINCA DE CAZULAS

Without question, the most popular walk in the **Almuñécar** region, this itinerary visits the **Junta de los Ríos** (the confluence of the **Ríos Verde** and **Negro**) then climbs along the **Río Verde**, taking in two fine *miradors*, a spectacular cable bridge, and countless plunge pools.

The traditional route is much longer, but the valley is prone to erosion and details further upstream can't be guaranteed from one winter to the next, let alone the lifetime of a book. However, despite being truncated, a paying route, and involving a long drive on a precipitous dirt track, the outing remains a must do for most holidaymakers.

Access: by car
Getting to the start is more adventurous than most walks. Access is via the **Finca de Cazulas** agricultural cooperative, the entrance to which is five kilometres north of **Otívar** at km42.4 of the A-4050, known locally as the **Carretera de la Cabra Montés** or mountain goat road, signposted 'Jete' and 'Otívar' from the centre of **Almuñécar**.

The entrance is shortly after the turning for the **Palacete de Cazulas**. In the summer months the gate is open from 10am to 7pm, Tuesdays to Sundays and there is an attendant in the toll booth. The cost, unchanged for many years, is 5 euros for the car and 5 euros per person. Children go free.

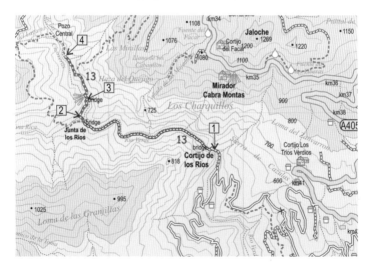

Between October and May, you have to telephone in advance and make an appointment for somebody to meet you at the gate. The number is 680 493 607. If there is no response on that number, you can also call 680 493 629.

Parking near the gorge's mouth

The call must be made in Spanish, so if you have no Spanish speakers in your party, ask the tourism office to arrange a rendezvous. The man from the cooperative will drive down with you to the second, locked gate and show you where to hide the key when you come back up. The top gate will be left unlocked, but bear in mind that they shut up shop at 19h.

To reach the start of the walk from the toll booth, fork right 100 metres from the top gate. Ignore a branch descending to the left at km2.2. 300 metres later, we come to the second gate. We can park just before the mouth of the gorge (which looks like it's sealed by a solid wall of rock from this perspective) at km4.5, immediately after the turning for the **Rijana Casa Rural**, or (if you're not too fussed about the state of your tyres) in the official parking areas at km0.5, km1.32, and km1.62 of the itinerary.

Thankfully, after such copious access details, the walk itself is very simple. Crossing a bridge at the entrance to the gorge (Wp.1 0M), we follow the dirt track along the right bank (our left) of the **Río Verde**, climbing gently under towering cliffs.

After two kilometres with no junctions and no distractions apart from the splendid isolation, we pass an iron footbridge which leads to a first plunge pool, if you're in a hurry to have a dip. Otherwise, we stay on the track until it ends at **Junta de los Ríos** 100 metres later, which is already a superb spot to visit (Wp.2 28M). The **Río Negro** is the branch to the left, the **Río Verde** is to the right.

The first stepping-stone ford

The second ford

Crossing the **Río Verde** via a stepping stone ford, we clamber over the eroded left bank (our right) for 100 metres to a second ford (old blue waymarks) composed of big boulders above a deep pool.

After a slightly acrobatic crossing, we join a broad trail leading to the first of the three cable bridges that were for many years the highlight of this itinerary (Wp.3 35M).

Cross one at a time and tell children (of whatever age) not to play silly buggers as the bridge is a bit bouncy – get a good rebound going and you could catapault yourself into the river!

That said, the best swimming pools on our short version of the standard itinerary are above and below this bridge, so if bouncing is your thing . . .

'bouncy' bridge

After the bridge, a steady climb precedes the first *mirador*. Thereafter, the steady climb continues on a stony path traversing a steep escarpment. Crossing a threshing circle high above the river, we pass a second even more spectacular *mirador* then descend back to the river (more bathing opportunities) and follow a rough, frequently waterlogged path up the left bank to the site of the second bridge (Wp.4 56M), only the site as the bridge itself was washed away when the river was in spate a few years ago.

The river can be forded here and theoretically it's still possible to continue upstream to the **Pozo Central**, a large pool below a spectacular waterfall. But this stretch is prone to erosion and the path further on is protected by rails that are flimsy to the point of non-existence, so I recommend turning back here. We return via the same route.

It's no accident that **Cerro Lopera** is topped by a firewatch hut: if you want fabulous views for minimum effort, this itinerary is hard to beat, a straightforward stroll up a shallow firebreak to one of the finest *miradors* in the *Parque Natural*. The route is wayposted, but waymarking, waypointing and description are largely superfluous as our objective, the firewatch hut, is within sight for most of the walk. There's a decent restaurant at km27 of the A-4050.

2 | 1H 20M | 5.5 km | | 200m / 200m | out & back | 3

Access: by car

Park near the ceramic sign to start

The walk starts at km28 of the A-4050, signposted 'Jete' and 'Otívar' from the centre of Almuñécar. There's no kilometre post, but the spot corresponds with the **Otívar** administrative limit, marked by a green ceramic sign, reading 'Gracias por su visita' on the southern side and 'Termino municipal Otívar' on the northern side.

The mapboard at Wp.1

The path (marked by a waypost and mapboard) is ten metres to the north on the western side of the road. There's room to park on either side of the road.

Cerro Lopera

From the mapboard (Wp.1 0M), we take the broad trail to the west, immediately bringing the **Sierra Nevada** into view behind us. 250 metres later, we cross a firebreak and stupendous views open out down toward the coast.

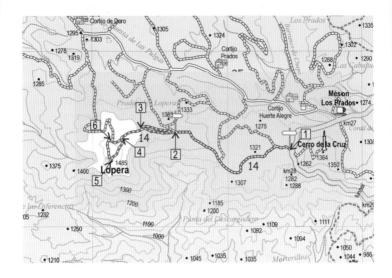

When the trail rejoins the firebreak 300 metres later, we simply follow the track along the back of the firebreak (SW, then W, then NW).

We soon start to climb, gently at first, then steadily, sticking with the firebreak as it veers left (W), passing a track and a trail branching off to the right within 50 metres of one another, the first of which has a waypost indicating we continue up the firebreak (Wp.2 21M).

Sierra Nevada views

When the trail and firebreak rejoin (Wp.3 28M), we veer left again (SW), following a rough track alongside the firebreak, crossing it again 300 metres later (Wp.4 33M) for the final climb to the trig point (Wp.5 38M). Down to the left, we can see the reservoir we visit in Walk 33.

We return the same way, except for a gentler descent we follow the fire warden's access track (NW) for 300 metres until it crosses the top of the firebreak, immediately after which we turn right on a cairn marked trail (Wp.6 45M), then take the branch trail between Wps.3&2.

Easy walking on broad trails and dirt tracks (except for one brief stretch of rough path at the end) traversing fine pine forest and exploring the peaceful countryside behind **Sedella**. The balcony path above **Río de la Fuente** is particularly beautiful and is a good spot for seeing *cabra montés*.

3 2H 50M 11.9 km 380m / 380m out & back 3

Access: by car
The walk starts from the *área recreativa/zona de acampada* west of **Sedella**, which can be reached by a steep, surfaced track, branching north from km5.3 of the MA-4105. The track is signposted 'Parque Natural' / 'Sendero Molino Los Pozuelos' and is opposite the turning for 'Los Valverdes' and 'Rubite'. The car park is 1.2km from the road.

The track to the recreation area

Our start from the car park (Wp.1)

From the top of the car park (Wp.1 0M), we take the wayposted dirt track forking right. 800 metres later, the dirt track doubles back to the left to pass between a byre and a water hut. Immediately behind the water hut (Wp.2 11M), we turn sharp right on a broad trail that climbs gently (NNE) before levelling off into a beautiful balcony path

The dirt track at Wp.3

high above **Río de la Fuente**. The walking is easy, but take care where you put your feet as the slope on the right is steep.

At the head of the valley, the path joins a dirt track (Wp.3 34M).

Doubling back to the left on the track, we resume climbing, still on a very gentle gradient.

A little over a kilometre later, we cross a firebreak, 300 metres after which we come to a junction of tracks (Wp.4 52M).

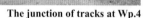

The junction of tracks at Wp.4

Bearing right, we pass a signboard marking an overgrown threshing circle. Climbing more steadily and crisscrossing the firebreak, we follow this track till it ends at the top of the firebreak in a turning circle on the **Collado de Monticara** (Wp.5 80M).

Immediately before the *collado*, a rough track branches off to the right. On the *collado*, there are two paths to the right.

Wp.5

The first, signposted 'Sendero Sedella La Maroma', does what is says on the label and is also used as a way of climbing **El Fuerte de Sedella**.

We take the second, narrower path, which is marked with a cairn, heading towards a large white sheet of rock, to the right of which we reach our destination, the splendidly named and splendidly located **Fuente La Pisaica del Niño Dios** (Wp.6 87M).

The ongoing path joins the **Sendero Casa de la Nieve** (Walks 27 & 35) climbing from **Canillas de Aceituno**, but for today we return by the same route.

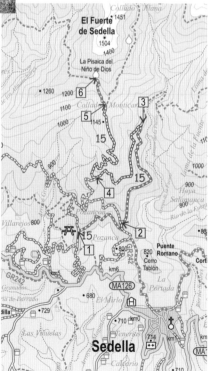

Our second itinerary starting from **Salares** features virtually everything that is most appealing about the Axarquía: a picture perfect village nestling in a lovely valley, wonderful woods, captivating paths, remote ruins, and fabulous views. Most of the walk coincides with the **GR249** and is clearly wayposted

Salares

| 3 | 2H | 7 km | 350m / 350m | | 3 |

Access: see Walk 1

Salares car park

The start of the walk is the same as Walk 1 except that at Wp.3 we carry straight on, following the **GR249** (Wp.3 6M).

The relevant waypoints are included in the waypoint file for the present itinerary.

Wp.2

Our path meanders up an attractive rocky gully, where we veer left at a junction (Wp.4 11M), the branch on the right being our return route.

Casa de la Haro

Traversing a beautiful cork oak forest, we enjoy great views back towards the village and up towards **La Maroma** (Walk 35), our path gradually bearing away from the **Río Salares** before bringing our next objective into view, the

white walls of a ruined *cortijo*,
Casa de la Haro.

A little over 1300 metres from
Wp.4, we cross a dry affluent
of the **Río Salares**, the **Arroyo
de Fogarate**, and climb to
Casa de la Haro (Wp.5 43M),
enjoying fine views.

Taking the rough dirt track to the left of the ruin, we climb gently then steadily
to a junction with a better stabilized track (Wp.6 54M), where we turn right,
still following the GR.

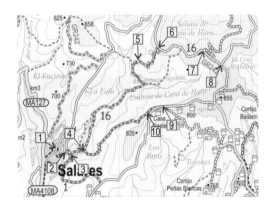

600 metres later, we ignore a branch forking left (Wp.7 61M) and continue on
the main track to a second junction at **Puerto de la Cruz del Muerto** (Wp.8
65M). Bearing right, we follow the GR onto the **Loma de Fogarate** ridge, a
majestic panorama opening out to north and south. We now simply stay on the
main track as it follows the back of the ridge, ignoring branch tracks accessing
enviably located houses.

After 800 metres, the track starts to descend gently. When it doubles back to
the left 300 metres later in front of **Casa Gante**, we leave both the main track
and the GR, carrying straight on behind **Casa Gante** (Wp.9 79M).

When this track in turn veers left and starts descending (Wp.10 82M), we
carry straight on again on a broad trail that descends back into the woods
before zigzagging down to rejoin our outward route at Wp.4 (103M).

For many years, the remote mountain villages of Spain had to make shift for themselves when it came to utilities, as a consequence of which many communities have a **Fábrica de la Luz**, literally a light factory, a small hydroelectric generating plant now superceded by the development of national services and converted into a leisure facility, taking advantage of picturesque riverside locations for camping zones and picnic areas. The best known of these in the Axarquía are those at **Cómpeta** (see Walk 8) and **Canillas de Albaida**. In this itinerary, we visit the latter via **Cerro Cueva del Agua**, the small mountain separating the *fábrica* from the village itself.

Access: on foot from Canillas

The village can be reached by bus from **Torre del Mar** (via **Cómpeta**) and by car via the same route. Our itinerary starts from the bus stop in front of the tourism office, where there's also room to park.

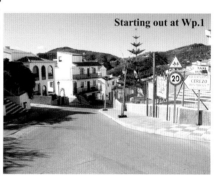

Starting out at Wp.1

From the bus stop (Wp.1 0M), we follow **Avenida de Andalucía** down past the pharmacy, then take **Calle Estación** past the bar/restaurant **Cerezo**.

We turn left when we see the brick archway

When we see the brick archway of the cemetery gates 250 metres later, we turn left (signposted 'Ruta Turistica al Pie, Paraje Natural, Fuente Santa, Río Llana') on a dirt tack passing behind the cemetery, ignoring the GR which descends to our left (Wp.2 5M).

At a Y-junction beyond the cemetery, we fork left (Wp.3 7M), away from **Finca Floretta**, and descend to another Y-junction with a broad trail (Wp.4 9M). Forking right, we follow the trail down to the **Río Llanada**, ignoring a branch to the left (Wp.5 12M) a little way above the river, which we cross by a stone footbridge.

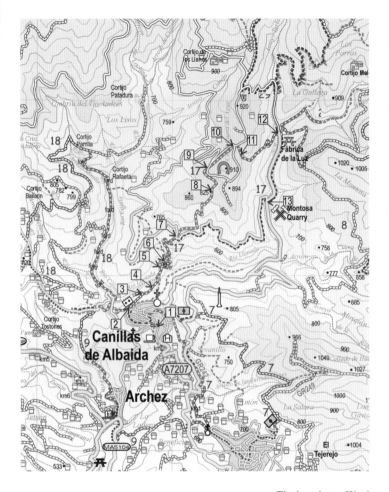

The junction at Wp.6

75 metres after the bridge, at a junction of signposted paths (Wp.6 15M), we double back to the right on the **Sendero Cerro del Agua / Fábrica de la Luz**. Following a clear path tracing out long traverses, we climb steadily through sparse pine forest to reach the lane we use on our return (Wp.7 34M)

Crossing the lane, we climb gently to steadily through pleasant pine woods. The path broadens to a trail that crosses a firebreak (Wp.8 50M) then, 300 metres later, a dirt track (Wp.9 55M). Beyond the track, we follow a narrower path parallel to the track, rejoining the firebreak 400 metres later (Wp.10 61M).

Crossing the firebreak and the track immediately below it, we take a broad, cairn-marked trail shadowing electricity lines, heading SE towards the Montosa quarry. The trail descends steeply then apparently peters out in a clearing to the right of the electricity lines (Wp.11 64M). However, on the far side of the clearing, a narrow path continues our descent, soon veering left to pass under the electricity lines and descend towards the northeast, initially on an exposed slope, subsequently shielded by trees.

Descending steeply on rough ground, we soon see the **Fábrica de la Luz**, which we reach via a ford below the riverside camping terrace.

The *área recreativa* is well maintained, equipped with toilets, picnic tables, barbecue bays, and a couple of springs.

The ford near the *fábrica*

From the car park (Wp.12 76M), we stroll down the access road (S) for 875 metres, passing the **Montosa** quarry, then double back to the right on a recently surfaced lane for 'Loma El Atajo, Hoya del Abad, Herrezuelas, Los Llanos' (Wp.13 86M). We follow this lane for just over two kilometres to rejoin our outward route at Wp.7 (110M).

18 CANILLAS DE ALBAIDA: CAMINO AL RÍO

When it comes to bucolics, the **Río Cajula** in **Canillas de Albaida** is about as good as it gets, a lovely little valley, lovingly tended by local fruit growers, irrigated by a lovely oleander lined stream, fronted by a lovely millhouse, and traversed by a lovely path. You get the picture, lovely all round. Most of the walk is well wayposted, so there's little need to consult the book en route.

We ford the river seven times, but the fords are easy and waterproof boots are not essential.

Access:
The walk starts from the **Puente Romano** millhouse at the confluence of the **Ríos Llanada** and **Cajula** just west of **Canillas de Albaida**.

*If you're staying in **Canillas** or arriving by bus*, from the tourism office bus stop, follow **Avenida de Andalucía** down past the pharmacy, then take **Calle Estación** past the bar/restaurant **Cerezo**. When you see the brick archway of the cemetery gates 250 metres later, turn left (signposted 'Ruta Turistica al Pie, Paraje Natural, Fuente Santa, Río Llana') then immediately left again, and follow the GR down a cobbled trail onto a minor road. The millhouse is 50 metres to the right.

If arriving by car, you can either park in the village and follow the directions above or stay on **Avenida de Andalucía** as it bypasses the old village centre then bear right at the junction with the **Árchez** road.

Park 500 metres later, either next to the 'Puente Romano' sign on the left immediately after the road bridge, or in the millhouse parking area on the right. Contrary to appearances, the latter is public land, but space is limited, so park carefully to avoid inconveniencing the owners of the mill and the people who tend the orchards in the valley.

Starting out at Wp.1

From the millhouse, we take the 'Ruta el Molino - Cruz del Muerto' path (Wp.1 0M) alongside the river to the left, traversing groves of citrus trees. 250 metres later, we ford the river and climb onto a terrace.

Strolling along the left bank (our right), we come to our second ford at the end of the citrus terraces.

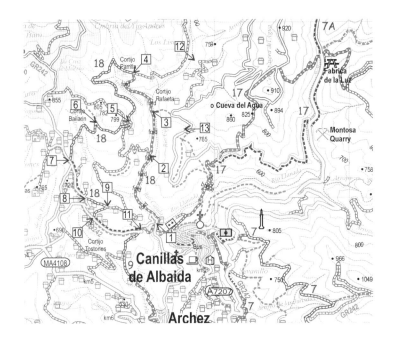

The ongoing path, which is intermittently cobbled, climbs gently to steadily before fording the river again and returning to citrus groves.

The junction at Wp.2

After the fourth ford, we climb across an avocado plantation to a junction with a dirt track below a ruin (Wp.2 15M). Bearing right ('Sendero, Camino Río'), we follow a narrow terrace path traversing the remainder of the avocado plantation onto the pine clad slopes of the *Parque Natural*.

Following a sandy path along the flank of the valley, we dip down to the fifth ford, and pass a branch path climbing to the right (Wp.3 25M).

Carrying straight on for 'Los Lisos, Cruz del Muerto', we cross our last significant ford 100 metres later.

The track at Wp.4

We now climb steadily along the southern flank of an affluent, which we cross at a virtually dry ford before joining a well-stabilized dirt track (Wp.4 39M).

Turning left for **Paraje los Lisos**, we follow this track for a long gentle climb until it joins the **GR242**, carrying straight on at a crossroads of tracks after 1500 metres (Wp.5 61M) and ignoring a cairn-marked path climbing to the right 400 metres after that (Wp.6 67M).

Views over the upper reaches of the valley

Our track joins the **GR242** on a surfaced lane below the **Fogarate** ridge (Wp.7 75M). Turning left and immediately forking left, we follow the GR all the way back to our starting point, though we can cut some road walking. 400 metres later, when the road winds through an S-bend between a line of houses, we can carry straight on down a dirt track behind the lower stretch of housing (signposted 'Cuevas') (Wp.8 81M) to a slanting T-junction (Wp.9 85M).

It is possible to descend directly to Wp.11 from here, but since the GR avoids the more direct route, I presume the rights of way haven't been clarified, so it's best to turn right to rejoin the road and the GR (Wp.10 88M). Turning left we descend to a sharp left hand bend, below which we turn right on a cobbled trail (Wp.11 95M) that brings us back to our starting point.

Eden Andalusian style: no snakes and apples, but affable farmers handing out the odd free orange (even by Andalusian standards the people hereabouts are exceedingly friendly) and a verdant valley overflowing with citrus fruits, medlars, quince, avocado, bananas, and I don't know what else. The walking is easy (much of it on surfaced track, all of it driveable, but none the less beguiling for that), the steep stretches punctuated by easy strolling and gentler gradients. There are no restaurants en route, but **Bar Cantero** in **Corumbuela** is extremely welcoming and about as authentic as it gets.

Access: by car
From the A-7206, take the western entrance into **Sayalonga**. Park beside the swimming pool and playground above **Fuente del Cid** (Wp.1).

From the playground parking bays (Wp.1 0M), we head into the village, signposted 'Meson Morisco, Musco de Nispero' (they're very proud of their medlars in **Sayalonga**), and 'Centro Urbano'. 230 metres later, in **Plaza de Andalucía**, we turn left on a brick stairway for **Cementerio Redondo** (the circular cemetery of which they are even prouder).

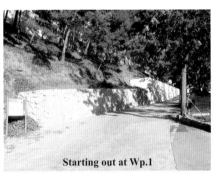

Starting out at Wp.1

Concrete lane and signboards at Wp.3

We now simply follow the signs for **Cementerio Redondo**, which we see off to our left after 400 metres (Wp.2 5M). Bearing left, we descend a concrete lane that doubles back to the right below the cemetery to the official trailhead, signposted 'Casa Rural, La Presa, El Molino, Corumbuela' (Wp.3 7M).

Throughout the itinerary there are countless turnings onto terraces and into private property, far too many to map at this scale, but happily they are nearly all obviously Not The Way, and to begin with all we have to remember is that we are descending to the **Río Cajula** via the main track, **Corumbuela** clearly visible up ahead of us.

Bridge over the Río Cajula

After passing to the right of a white reservoir (Wp.4 12M), we descend a long stretch of concrete that subsequently follows the river before crossing it via an attractive stone bridge, above which we pass the imposing **Casa Balcón de Río** and **Casa El Molino**.

Climbing out of the lush, lower reaches of the valley, we traverse drier slopes dotted with almond, carob, and olive trees.

Sticking to the main track, we climb steadily and occasionally steeply. After a long level stretch passing **Finca las Brisa** and **Finca Almendra**, we join the bend of another track (Wp.5 55M), where we bear left and carry on climbing, bringing into view the mountains behind **Cómpeta**.

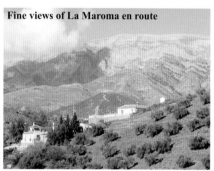

Fine views of La Maroma en route

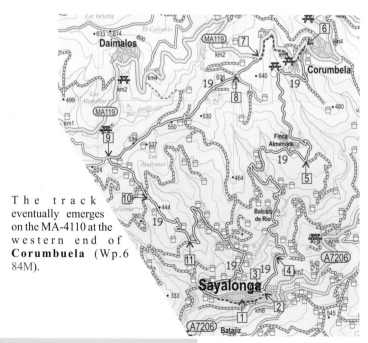

The track eventually emerges on the MA-4110 at the western end of **Corumbuela** (Wp.6 84M).

Our return route follows the road to the left, but first it's worth exploring **Corumbuela**, above all the very welcoming **Bar Cantero**, to reach which we take the paved lane directly in front of us for 100 metres, then turn left at the junction with **Calle Axarquía**. Otherwise, we follow the road west, climbing for a little over a kilometre.

When the road starts to descend, we fork left (Wp.7 99M) on a broad track behind a *cortijo*. Again, the rule is 'Follow the main track ignoring all branches', with the additional stipulation of 'Carry straight on'. All we have to do is identify the turning at Wp.9.

We first apply the carry-straight-on rule 300 metres from the road, where we ignore a major branch on the left and head southwest, apparently away from **Sayalonga** (Wp.8 103M). Carrying straight on at every junction, we follow this track for nearly two kilometres, bringing into view the attractive, little-visited village of **Arenas** off to our right.

After one and a half kilometres, we pass below a villa with a square belvedere. 400 metres later, we turn left on a track (concreted for the first 200 metres) marked with old yellow and new green waymarks (Wp.9 127M) passing above a new villa.

Our concrete track, Wp.9

.. passing above a new villa

Heading towards **Sayalonga**, the carry-straight-on ignore-minor-branches rule resumes, notably at the bottom of a long stretch of concrete (Wp.10 134M), where we ignore the track doubling back to the right and instead climb briefly past two *casetas*.

After descending steeply past **Villa Peña Blanca**, we ignore a major branch doubling back to the right (Wp.11 146M). Passing **Finca La Hoya** and **Cortijo Pepe y Angelina**, we descend to a concrete ford then climb a concrete lane back to Wp.1.

The Costa del Sol is dotted with *rábitas*, small conical summits that are the culminating points of the coastal ridges. Among the best known is **La Rábita de Torrox**, which stands midway between **Torrox** and **Cómpeta**, and enjoys the sort of commanding sea views that estate agents dream about.

Consequently, this is not a walk for those who prize wilderness. There are houses everywhere. But they're not the sort of houses to be sniffy about and the panorama is never less than splendid, so if you like easy walking on good tracks with stunning vistas, this is the itinerary for you.

Access: by car
The walk starts at km7.6 of the A-7207, a sharp left hand bend (approached from the south) with a dirt track on the right signposted 'Acebuchal, Zona Recreativa Fábrica de la Luz' and 'La Ruta del Acebuchal'. Park on the broad dirt platform at the start of the **Acebuchal** track. If you don't have your own transport, the starting point can be reached on foot from **Cómpeta** via Walk 8 Wps.1-7.

The start at Wp.1

From the **Acebuchal** junction (Wp.1 0M), we walk back down the road towards **Torrox** (S) for 50 metres, then take the roughly metalled track climbing steeply to the left. The metalling gives way to dirt 100 metres later (surfaces shift between concrete, tarmac and dirt so frequently on this

Pavo Real (Wp.2)

itinerary that I shall no longer mention them unless helpful for identifying the route), after which the track descends on the far side of the hill to rejoin the A-7207 at the bar/restaurante **Pavo Real** (The **Royal Turkey**, which obviously doesn't have quite the same ring to it in English) (Wp.2 17M).

We turn left here, following the road for 50 metres, then bear left again on another intermittently metalled track climbing steadily toward the summit of **La Rábita**. At a large concrete reservoir (Wp.3 24M), we ignore the dirt branch to the left (our return route) and carry straight on, climbing a steeply raked concrete track, passing to the left of a line of houses, among them the aptly named **El Escalador**. 50 metres after **El Escalador**, the track levels off and stunning sea views open out to the west.

After following a contour below the summit, we join another track (Wp.4 41M) where we bear left. Passing between a large house and another large reservoir, we descend toward a cluster of half a dozen houses, the nearest of which has a glass atrium. Joining an asphalted lane below the houses (Wp.5 51M), we turn left, then double back to the left in front of the house with the atrium (House '010B'), which is fronted by a rank of grape-drying beds.

Our track at Wp.7

Following a narrow dirt track, we descend to a Y-junction (Wp.6 57M). The branch on the left accesses a platform beside a slightly higgledy-piggledy house.

We bear right, then right again below the higgledy-piggledy

Fine views of the summits to the north

house and keep descending for 500 metres until we come to a junction with a dirt track doubling back to the left (Wp.7 69M).

Turning left, we follow this track until it rejoins our outward route at Wp.3 (102M), enjoying superb views of the sierra's high summits, including **El Fuerte** (Walk 31), **Lucero** (Walk 36), and **Alto de Cielo** (Walk 38).

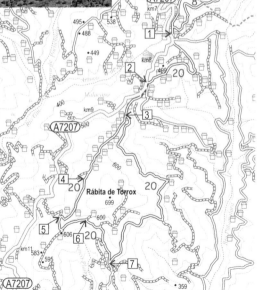

73

Our other **Acebuchal** itineraries (Walks 3 & 8) are very domestic, sticking to broad trails and good dirt tracks. This itinerary is more adventurous, taking us into the wild, untenanted land around **Loma de la Mata** and **Cerro Verde**. Pathfinding requires a modicum of attention (notably at Wps.3 & 6), but it's worth it to get off the beaten track and enjoy some great views. Long trousers are preferable though not essential between Wps.3&6.

Access: by car
Acebuchal can be reached via **Frigiliana** or from the A-7207 between **Cómpeta** and **Torrox**. Both involve driving on dirt track. To minimize this, the **Frigiliana** approach is preferable (1.7km of track as opposed to 6.5 from the west). Whether driving or walking to the start, see Walk 3 (Wps.1-3) and Walk 8 (Wps.7-9) for details. Park in the broad cutting beside **Capilla San Antonio** at the southern end of **Acebuchal** (Wp.1).

From the **Capilla San Antonio** car park (Wp.1 0M), we take the track to the south descending gently to **Acebuchal Bajo**. After the lower hamlet, we climb gently to a platform on a U-bend, where a path branches left toward the **Rábita de Torrox** (Walk 20) (Wp.2 21M).

Parking and Wp.1

Take this narrow cairn-marked path (Wp.3)

From this point we can see, tucked into the **Patamalara** valley to the north, part of the old electricity installations at the bottom of the valley and, on the western flank, a small white building roofed with dull red tiles, behind which there is a tiny white cabin. *This is an important point of reference for finding the path up **Loma de la Mata**.* As we continue along the track, the white building disappears from view. 300 metres after we lose sight of it, the red roof of the main building and the walls of the cabin are visible again, at which point we fork right on a narrow path flanked by cairns (Wp.3 31M).

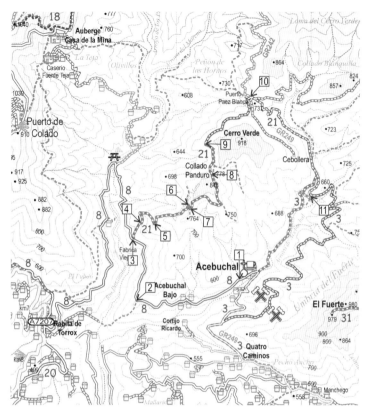

If the full building comes back into view, you've gone too far. If approaching from the west, this turning is 4.2 kilometres from the A-7207.

Climbing steadily amid broom, palm, cistus, and huge bushes of rosemary, we reach the head of a dry watercourse where there's a large cairn (Wp.4 38M). Ignoring a very faint way branching left, we bear right. The path almost immediately resumes its northerly course, still climbing steadily, until views open out up the valley and the path veers east then southeast to climb towards a crest, where we emerge on a small plateau overlooking **Torrox** (Wp.5 50M).

Bearing left (N), we head toward two small conical summits on Loma de la Mata. These mini summits are another important point of reference as it's easy to stray off path directly below them. Immediately below the two summits, we reach two Y-junctions within five metres of each other (Wp.6 63M). Doubling back to the right, we climb (SE) toward a solitary pine tree 40 metres away on the saddle between the two conical summits.

At the pine tree (Wp.7), we veer left to follow a clear path curling round the eastern flank of the *loma* to the **Collado Panduro** below **Cerro Verde** (Wp.8 79M), where a pathless, cairn-marked route branches right toward the summit. Sticking with the main path, we follow a contour round the western flank of **Cerro Verde**, traversing a series of run-off channels where there's a very slight risk of vertigo.

75

Beyond the run-off channels, our path runs into the end of an abandoned dirt track, now largely reduced to a broad trail (Wp.9 90M), which joins the **GR249** at a crossroads of tracks on **Puerto de Paez Blanca** (Wp.10 100M).

The track after Wp.9

Turning right, we follow the GR back to **Acebuchal**, descending along the track until it runs into and then climbs out of the **Arroyo Acebuchal**, 100 metres above which, at a junction marked by cairns and wayposts (Wp.11 121M), we turn right to descend into the dry riverbed, returning to the start via Walk 3 (Wps.4-3).

22

Combining three official itineraries, this walk visits one of **Frigiliana**'s finest *miradors*, **Cerro Felix** on the **Sierra de Enmedio** between the **Ríos Chillar** and **Higuerón**, incorporating en route the most spectacular stretch of Walk 2. You need to have an eye for a path as the ways along **Sierra de Enmedio** are obscure, despite their enduring popularity, but it's worth it as the views are remarkable for such a relatively low altitude.

Don't venture into the **Higuerón** gorge after, during, or when there is a threat of heavy rain.

Starting at Wp.1

Access: see Walk 10

We start as per Walk 2, Wps.1 to 4, which are included in the waypoint file for the present itinerary.

When the valley broadens after the *cahorros* and the riverbed is crossed by a track (Wp.4 38M), we leave Walk 2 and instead turn left. The track, which is surfaced with concrete above the embankment, climbs steeply then steadily, passing a branch accessing houses on the left.

The main track then levels off before descending slightly to a second left-hand branch, this one signposted 'Parque Natural' and 'Quinto Pino' (Wp.5 51M), at which point we intersect with Walk 32.

Wp.5, intersecting with Walk 32

Turning left and ignoring two rough branch tracks that immediately fork left and right, we follow the central concrete branch for 200 metres up to the **Quinto Pino** villa, behind which we carry straight on along a rough dirt track.

At the junction 300 metres later (Wp.6 60M), we take the right-hand fork, a narrower, stonier track closed to traffic by a metal cable. Climbing gently along the perimeter of the *Parque Natural*, we pass the partially interred remains of a limekiln before bringing into view **Lucero** (Walk 36) then **Alto de Cielo** (Walk 38). The track levels off as we skirt **Cerro Pinto** (Walk 32), passing a second better preserved limekiln before reaching a Y-junction behind **Cerro Pinto** (Wp.7 75M). Forking left then immediately right, we take the stony path running along the ridge of **Sierra de Enmedio** (N), fabulous views opening out over the **Río Chillar**.

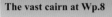

The vast cairn at Wp.8

Y-junction, Wp.7

When the path splinters after 30 metres, we take the lower, clearer traces, briefly dropping down onto the western flank of the ridge.

Keeping an eye out for the occasional cairns and red waymarks, we wind along the ridge, passing a vast cairn on a small saddle (Wp.8 89M), beyond which the path steepens for its final steady but

Wp.9, Cerro Felix summit

comparatively brief slog up to the cairn-capped summit of **Cerro Felix** (Wp.9 105M).

Carrying straight on, we descend steeply on a slightly skittery path onto the back of the *cerro*.

Ignoring a minor fork to the left, we skirt a small knoll, joining Walk 10 and the **GR249** fifty metres later (Wp.10 116M). Turning left, we descend back into the **Higuerón** riverbed, where we bear left again to rejoin our outward route at Wp.2 (125M).

23

The walk up the **Río Chillar** (most of it *in* the river) and through the metre wide straits of the *cahorros* is probably the Axarquía's most celebrated adventure and certainly the most spectacular excursion accessible to all walkers regardless of experience or fitness. All you need is a pair of sandals and a penchant for splashing about - a strong penchant because we splash about a lot and it can be quite exhausting.

Exertion ratings and timings are extremely relative depending on where you turn back and the level of water. We've done it ankle-to-calf deep and it was a doddle. Calf-to-thigh deep was a little less doddley and a bit more doddery. There are some superb spots to be explored upriver, but this is very much a cut your coat to suit your cloth job. Turn back before fatigue compels it. River splashing fun is no fun at all when you're tired.

Due to poor GPS reception, the distance and climb are estimated and should be regarded as rough guidelines. The cleft exertion rating and global time reflect the very variable conditions. Do not even think of venturing into the *cahorros* after, during, or when there is a threat of heavy rain.

Access:
On foot from **Nerja**. Parking is prohibited at the traditional starting point (Wp.3), a prohibition that is enforced in the summer months.

If arriving by car, take the N340 into **Nerja** from the **Maro** end, passing the 'Mercadona/Supersol' roundabout. At the next roundabout (**Burriana** on the left, 'Centro Salud' on the right), get into the slip lane parallel to the main road. 75 metres later, turn right and follow **Calle Picasso** to the river, on the nearside of which (600 metres from the roundabout) it crosses a dirt track (marked with a GR X-post to our right) where there's plenty of room to park (Wp.1).

If arriving by bus, directly behind **Nerja** bus station take **Calle Joaquin Herrera** which descends past a 'dead end' sign onto a concrete trail joining the riverbed track. Turn right to reach Wp.1 800 metres later when the track crosses an asphalted lane.

Starting at Wp.1

Motorists can (in theory) park closer to Wp.3, though I have had reports of this car park being closed. From the **Burriana** roundabout (see above), take the Centro Salud turning on the right and follow **Avenida de la Constitución** for one kilometre to a distinctive red house on your left, behind which in **Calle Mirto** there is a large car park. From the car park, walk down **Calle Mirto** then fork right to follow a concrete track to Wp.3.

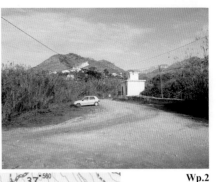

Wp.2

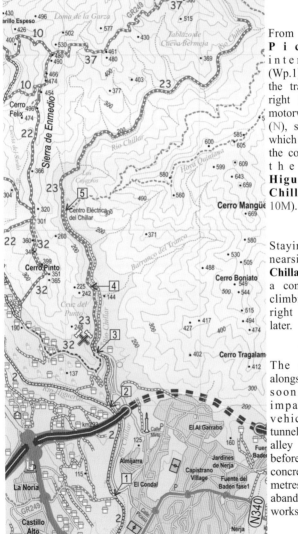

From the **Calle Picasso** intersection (Wp.1), we take the track on the right toward the motorway viaduct (N), shortly after which we come to the confluence of the **Ríos Higuerón** and **Chillar** (Wp.2 10M).

Staying on the nearside of the **Chillar**, we ignore a concrete track climbing to the right 75 metres later.

The dirt track alongside the river soon becomes impassable to vehicles as it tunnels through an alley of bamboo before joining the concrete track 100 metres short of an abandoned cement works.

When the surfaced track doubles back to the left for 'Los Almáchares' at the cement works (Wp.3 17M), we carry straight on along a stony track following the broad bed of the river below the old quarry. 800 metres later, we pass to the left of a white concrete cabin perched on a broad pedestal (Wp.4 26M).

Wp.3

The perched cabin, Wp.4

You can expect to start walking in water here, though you may be able to keep your feet dry for another kilometre until we pass the old generating plant (Wp.5 44M).

Wet or dry, this is where we stow both book and GPS (reception is poor after the generating plant), as there's no going wrong and it's just a question of keeping on keeping on until we decide we've had enough.

Where you turn back is for you to decide, but to give you an idea of what to expect, we climb a concrete ramp (slippery when wet) and continue upstream, now emphatically in the water. After about 25 minutes, we reach the first modest stretch of *cahorros* (72M). We then make our way through two very spectacular *cahorros* (82M & 97M).

Progress becomes increasingly arduous after this point and most people turn back at the *cahorros*, but if you're up for it, it's worth continuing, as a little over an hour later we reach a series of deep pools and rapids that precede a succession of fine waterfalls (177M to 182M). By this time, all but the most hydrophiliac will have had enough.

We return the same way.

Negotiating the *cahorros*

The **Pinarillo** *área recreativa* north of **Maro** is a popular picnic spot traditionally used as the springboard for routes up the **Barranco de Cazadores**, including **Navachica** (the **Sierra de Almijara**'s highest summit) and the **Tajo del Almendrón**. Due to erosion on the old mining path up the *barranco*, these walks are not recommended. However, **Pinarillo** is still worth visiting and on this short itinerary we explore the hills overlooking it from the east.

A *tajo* is a sheer cliff face, a definition you will appreciate when you see the **Tajos del Sol** and **Almendrón** en route. **Tajo Baena** is an altogether more modest affair, but the views from the top are great and there's every chance you will see *cabra montés* nonchalantly strolling about above precipitous drops. We, however, take no chances. The path is well made, unmistakable, and studiously avoids anything vertiginous.

Access: by car
From exit 295 of the A7, follow the signs to 'Cuevas de Nerja'. At the entrance to the car park, take the 'Área Recreativa El Pinarillo / Fuente del Esparto' dirt track, setting the odometer at 0. Park at the junction of tracks at km2.9, signposted on the right 'Sendero' (Walk 38) and straight ahead 'Area Recreativa El Pinarillo 2km'. If you don't want to drive on dirt track or don't have your own transport, you can join the present itinerary 200 metres after Wp.1 by following Walk 4.

From the junction at km2.9 (Wp.1 0M), we continue along the main track, following the **GR249** for 'Pinarillo', passing a branch doubling back to the left 200 metres later (Wp.4 of Walk 4) and a second minor branch off to the left 450 metres further on (Wp.2 7M).

Wp.1

Tajo del Amendrón

After the second branch, look up ahead and you will see two summits on the western ridge defining the **Barranco de Cazadores**. The more distant is the **Tajo del Sol**, the nearer the **Tajo del Almendrón**.

Tajo Baena

Off to our right, we can see the cliffs of **Tajo Baena** and the two small summits we pass on our descent.

Wp.3, at the recreation area

At the *área recreativa* (Wp.3 22M), we leave the GR, which swings left to cross the car park in front of the kiosk bar, and instead continue on the track for 'Fuente Esparto 2km'. When the track veers left a kilometre later (Wp.4 34M), we bear right into **Barranco de Cazadores.**

Bearing right at Wp.4

50 metres into the *barranco* (Wp.5), we fork right on a cairn marked path, and that's really all you need to know, as there are no junctions during the traverse of **Tajo Baena**.

We climb steeply toward **Alto de Cielo** (Walk 38), pausing to contemplate the splendid views up **Barranco de Cazadores**.

Pinarillo, seen from the summit

After 400 metres, the path swings south and the gradient eases briefly before steepening again, bringing into view the first summit crags, which we cross after a final steady to steep climb (Wp.6 62M).

83

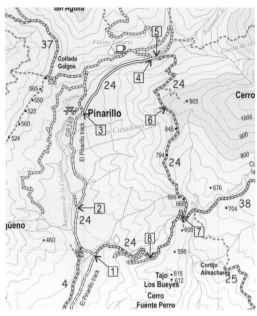

100 metres later, we pass behind a second rocky outcrop, where superb views open out over the sea and we begin our equally unequivocal descent.

Descending to the left of a third, less craggy hummock, we head toward the pyramid like summit of **Tajo de los Bueyes** (SSE), bringing into view the **Cortijo de la Civila** dirt track and, down to our right, our starting point.

After a steady, occasionally skittery descent, we join the **Cortijo de la Civila** dirt track at Wp.3 of Walk 38 (Wp.7 84M).

Turning right, we follow the track back to the starting point, taking advantage of three shortcut paths, the first of which, marked with a waypost, comes 900 metres later (Wp.8 94M).

The second is directly below the end of the first, the third 20 metres to the left at the end of the second.

The first of the shortcut paths (Wp.8)

25

A classic climb taking in a tranquil ravine, great views, and a picturesque ruin. Also a useful itinerary for piecing together longer outings, with obvious links to Walks 4, 24, & 38 (see Wp.LINK). Experience suggests that the **Barranco Sanguino** is always dry, nonetheless, the usual provisos about walking in riverbeds after, during, or when there is a threat of heavy rain still apply.

Access: On foot from Maro

Wp.1 is the 'Playa/Cala del Maro' roundabout at the eastern end of the village. If arriving by car, the car park is 100 metres down the 'Playa' road. If arriving by bus, from the the bus stop, take the main road through **Maro** to the roundabout.

The Playa roundabout (Wp.1)

From the Playa roundabout (Wp.1 0M), we walk up to the N340 and take the tunnel under the motorway, bearing left on a lane leading to smallholdings and houses. When the asphalt ends, we continue on the concrete riverbed track until the gates of a private house (Wp.2 8M), where we fork right into the

stony bed of **Barranco Sanguino**. We now embark on a delightful stroll up the *barranco*, our trail shaded by tall pine trees, the motorway nothing but a distant rumour behind us, the silence soon absolute apart from the chirping of birds and any chatty companions you may have with you.

We fork right at Wp.2

There's no call for consulting a book here, but for the purposes of pacing progress, we pass a fire blackened cave, shortly after which we ignore paths branching left and right (Wp.3 16M).

Traversing ever more remote terrain, we pass a very faint way on our left (imperceptible were it not for a cairn) (Wp.4 21M). We then pass twin motorbike trails climbing steeply to the right (Wp.5 26M). A kilometre later, the valley begins to broaden and we catch glimpses off to our left of the craggy cliffs defining **Tajo de los Bueyes**.

Our stony trail at Wp.6

When the cliffs are directly in front of us (albeit largely obscured by the trees), we leave the *barranco*, taking a broad, stony path, clearly marked with cairns, climbing to the right (Wp.6 46M).

Cortijo Almáchares

Climbing steadily (E) amid a sea of rosemary, we double back to the right at a cairn marked junction with a faint branch that carries straight on (Wp.7 54M), after which the white walls of our destination, the ruined **Cortijo Almáchares**, come into view up to our left.

Looking south from the *cortijo*

Reaching a T-junction (Wp.8 68M), we turn left for the final climb to a junction directly behind the *cortijo* (Wp.9 89M). On the far side of the ruin, there's a threshing circle, a good spot for a picnic.

The path continuing to the north joins the **Cortijo de la Civila** dirt track 800 metres later (Wp.LINK) just east of Walk 24 Wp.7 & Walk 38 Wp.3.

We return by the same route.

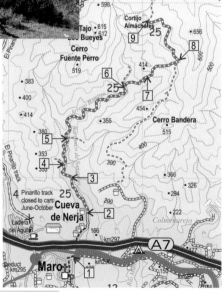

Cantarriján is the last cove in the **Maro-Cerro Gordo Paraje Natural** that non-residents can reach by car. Blessed with a great beach, rugged hills, grand sea views, limpid waters, and two excellent *chiringuitos* (seafront fish restaurants), this is an essential Costa del Sol outing, and even if you find off path walking off putting, it's worth visiting for a stroll to the **Torre de Caleta**, carrying straight on at Wp.3 then turning left at Wp.10.

The traverse of **Cerro Caleta** is an exception to our 'no off path' rule as it's a popular classic on which orientation is easy, the way defined by cliffs on one side and a steep escarpment on the other. Off path timings are more than usually subjective and you should allow up to an hour for the stretch between Wps.3 & 6, certainly longer than the 'moving time' recorded here. There's a slight risk of vertigo between Wps.3 & 4.

Access: by car

Take the 'Playa de Cantarriján' turning at the 'La Herradura Costa Tropical' provincial limit on the N340 between **Maro** and **La Herradura**. Park at km1.1 (Wp.2) or at the beach (Wp.1) (in the restaurant car park if eating there or the public car park behind it if not).

From the western end of the beach (Wp.1 0M), we walk up the dry riverbed parallel to the access lane for 400 metres.

Wp.1, at the western end of the beach

When the riverbed levels off alongside the lane, GR waymarks on a large, partially interred rock on our left indicate where we double back to the left on a narrow path (Wp.2 6M, see photo on the next page) climbing steadily onto the headland above **Cantarriján**.

The rock indicating our path at Wp.2

325 metres later, **Nerja** comes into view (Wp.3 11M), at which point we leave the main path, turning right on a rough way heading inland (NNW). After a steady to steep climb (waymarked with occasional cairns and frequent blue dots), we reach the culminating

Views down to Playa Cantarriján

point of the walk on the ridge behind (well behind!) the **Cerro Caleta** cliffs (Wp.4 25M), from where we have superb views all along the coast and inland toward **Alto de Cielo** (Walk 38).

We now follow the ridge (N), keeping an eye out for the waymarks and staying well back from the cliffs. Toward the end of the main ridge, a clearer path resolves itself amid the scrub (Wp.5 34M), dipping up and down before descending steeply to a shrine to **Saint Judas Tadeo**, below which we join the **Playa Cañuelo** dirt track (Wp.6 48M).

Views from the high point of our route

Turning left, we descend past two left-hand turnings, a track and a trail, both leading to private property, and a track branching right to reach holiday homes (Wp.7 53M). Sticking with the main track, we descend to the beach (Wp.8 64M). Turning left, we follow the track to the eastern end of the beach, passing the **Chiringuito Las Piedras** and apparently heading for a dead end. In fact, in the far nook of the beach, we find a rough path (Wp.9 69M) climbing steeply (better up than down!) onto a terrace behind the **Peñón del Fraile** headland and the diminutive **Playa de las Doncellas**, where you have to watch your step as the terrace path is prone to erosion.

We then zigzag up to pass between the **Caleta** cliffs and the **Punta de Caleta** martello tower, the latter a five minute detour off the main path at the clear junction we reach after contouring round a deep gully (Wp.10 78M). Otherwise, we continue on the main path to the left, rejoining our outward route at Wp.3 (90M).

Circling a really spectacular lump of rock, this glorious itinerary takes us into a world of perfect peace where the noisiest thing you're likely to encounter is the fabulously turbulent *barranco* architecture above the **Tajos Lisos**. It's a wonderful wild route traversing remote terrain without ever being risky and the views are stupendous. The first stretch follows the **Sendero Casa de la Nieve**, the snow gatherers' path that is the classic ascent of **La Maroma** (Walk 35). *Expect to be out for at least five hours.*

Access: on foot from Canillas See Walk 6 for details.

From **Canillas** car park (Wp.1 0M), we follow the main road into the village, bearing left into a small plaza 140 metres later in front of the **Asador La Maroma**. At the far end of the plaza, a steep path and stairway climb to a junction beside house Nº38, where we turn right, then immediately fork left to reach twin stairways, at the top of which are signs for 'Sendero Casa de la Nieve' and 'La Rábita' (Wp.2 6M).

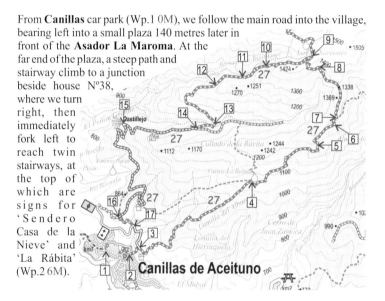

Our path up to the right (Wp.3)

Turning right then left 50 metres later, we take another series of steps climbing out of the village onto a rough path passing between two byres, behind which we reach a triple junction of dirt tracks (Wp.3 10M). Up to the right, on the higher of the two right hand branches, a waypost and mapboard mark the start of our path.

The path above Wp.3

Taking the upper fork on the right and immediately branching left, we leave the track, and follow a broad trail climbing steadily above the village, the less spectacular eastern flank of **Peñón Grande** visible off to our left. After crossing patches of ancient cobbling amid scattered pine and some lovely karstic glades, we traverse scrubland clad with cistus and broom.

After a long, steady slog (NE) on an increasingly abraded trail, the **Tajos de la Capellania** cliffs below **La Maroma** come into view, and the way more or less levels out amid a stand of pine, where we cross a sheet of rock, beyond which a narrow path passes behind **Fuente La Rábita** (Wp.4 49M). 50 metres to the right, in front of a shallow cave, we resume our steady northeasterly ascent, **La Maroma** disappearing from view as we traverse a more austere landscape enlivened by fine views and occasional sightings of *cabra montés*.

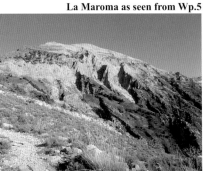
La Maroma as seen from Wp.5

After a long northeasterly climb, we cross the **Lomilla de Albercón** spur where there's a large cairn (Wp.5 74M) and the main bulk of **La Maroma** comes back into view. Following a rocky way punctuated with cairns, we skirt the impressive **Barranco de los Almanchares**, toward the top of which we reach a junction marked with a flurry

The rock at Wp.7

of cairns and a line of stones across the path heading toward the *barranco* (Wp.6 82M). Doubling back to the left, we stay on the main trail, which passes another branch path off to the right 150 metres later (Wp.7 85M), the latter marked with a rock daubed with old red paint indicating 'Canillas' back the way we've come and 'Buitre' off to the right.

Near the head of the *barranco*, our trail veers northwest, crossing a small col, after which we can see the end of a dirt track down to our left. This is the track we take back to **Canillas**. For the present, we continue along the **Casa de la Nieve** path, which is pleasantly shady at this point, following a contour line crossing a watercourse with a tiny cement dam forming a drinking trough (Wp.8 98M). Thereafter, the climbing resumes, bringing us onto the back of a stony spur, the **Collado de los Charcones**, fifty metres along which we reach a Y-junction (Wp.9 109M), which is where the present itinerary and Walk 35 diverge.

The left-hand branch (Wp.9)

Ignoring the wayposted branch on the right, we fork left on a narrow stony path descending along the left bank of the **Barranco de Tajos Lisos**. After following a contour line for 200 metres, the path drops down to a lower contour, where the route is slightly overgrown but sufficiently well used to remain clear.

A gentle, intermittently skittery descent waymarked with occasional cairns takes us past an old limekiln (Wp.10 121M), after which we descend more steadily into increasingly wild and remote terrain, where we approach the **Tajos Lisos** watercourse, a few metres above which we pass a waypost (Wp.11 129M).

Staying on the southern side of the stream, we climb briefly on a broader trail then follow a contour line, passing another limekiln (Wp.12 133M). The path swings away from the main ravine and descends to the south before veering east to reach an affluent, where there's a concrete reservoir and a third limekiln (Wp.13 146M). Crossing the affluent, we climb to the dirt track seen from above, where there's a signboard for 'La Maroma' (Wp.14 148M). We follow this track for the next three and a half kilometres, virtually all the way back to the village.

Peñón Grande

Bearing right, we start descending, gently at first then more steeply through a series of long chicanes. On the cusp of the first chicane, we pass the **Mirador de Castillejo** (Wp.15 160M), a natural *mirador* with some stunning views. A little over 700 metres later, we pass through a narrow defile and **Canillas** comes into view.

We now descend towards the roofless walls of an unfinished and clearly abandoned building, beyond which the track veers away from **Canillas**, then curves south. 75 metres after a wayposted path on our right, we turn left on a shortcut path (Wp.16 185M) and descend steadily to join a branch track above the village (Wp.17 189M). Turning left, we rejoin our outward route at Wp.3.

Acclaimed by one local company as the best *mirador* in the park, **Cerro Verde** lives up to both its reputation and its name, being one of the few genuinely green peaks hereabouts, the nominative claims of other summits notwithstanding.

The approach (which is waymarked until Wp.5) is particularly peaceful and remote. The descent between Wps.6&8 is rough and adventurous (though never vertiginous), therefore not recommended when visibility is poor, but otherwise it makes for a lovely combination of the wild and the domestic, leading as it does to an easy stroll on dirt track.

If you don't like the look of this descent or visibility is poor, return the same way from the summit. The full loop is a useful recce if you are considering driving to **Puerto Blanquillo** to do Walk 36 as the present itinerary uses a long stretch of the access track.

Access: by car
The itinerary starts at the **Canillas de Albaida Fábrica de la Luz** (Walk 17). The *fábrica* access lane is signposted from the eastern end of **Canillas**. Take the signposted branch to the right, setting the odometer at zero. 400 metres later, at the top of the village, turn right, then fork left at km1.7. The *fábrica* is 3.6km from the entrance to the village. If you don't have your own transport, there's a taxi service in **Canillas** (T. 699 933 026). If you take this option, you might consider staying on the dirt track at Wp.2 on the return to walk back to the village. Wp.2 is a little under seven kilometres from the village, which would make for a long day, but the walking is easy.

From the southern end of the **Fábrica de la Luz** car park, we take the chained access ramp (Wp.1 0M) onto the upper terraces of the *zona de acampada*, then double back to the right 25 metres later on a path (waymarked with a green dot) that climbs past a fire hazard warning sign.

Our start point (Wp.1)

Climbing steadily, we zigzag up to cross a dry *acequia* 300 metres later. Above the *acequia*, we weave through the woods on a broad trail, climbing to join the track between **Canillas** and **Puerto Blanquillo** (Wp.2 24M).

Turning left and ignoring a branch descending to the left 40 metres later, we climb gently along the track, passing the bottom of the firebreak we traverse later on. After 1200 metres on the track (Wp.3 40M), we reach **Fuente Borrequero**, a spring with a large concrete trough, from where we can see the

rocky outcrop of **Cerro Verde**'s neighbour, **Cerro Atalaya**. Turning right, we follow a clear path climbing steadily along the right bank (our left) of the dry gully above the *fuente*, crossing onto the left bank just below another spring 150 metres later.

Following a narrow path carpeted with pine needles, we continue climbing steadily alongside the watercourse, then gradually veer away from it (S) to climb steeply toward the firebreak. The path eventually runs alongside the firebreak for 175 metres before joining it (Wp.4 58M) below the *atalaya* crags.

The col overlooking the sea Wp.5

Lucero comes into view

Cerro Atalaya

Bearing left, we follow the ridge for 100 metres to the end of the firebreak where the path resumes, climbing gently along the left flank of the *atalaya* to a T-junction on a col overlooking the sea (Wp.5 71M).

The green route we have been following so far turns right here for a largely pathless ascent of the *atalaya*, but we turn left, bringing **Lucero** (Walk 36) into view.

The trig point

Climbing steadily to steeply, we follow a shoulder of **Cerro Verde** (NNE) onto the splendid little eerie of the pine fringed summit. The trig point (Wp.6 90M) is reached either by climbing off path through the wood directly behind it, or by contouring round to its eastern end, where a very faint way doubles back to the right.

At first glance, there's no route east from here, but 100 metres northeast of the trig point on the northern flank of the mountain, we pick up the head of a clear path, confirmed by a cairn a little over 100 metres further on (Wp.7 97M). From this point, we can see a narrow saddle below us, the **Blanquillo** track down to our left, and (at the far end of the saddle, just before the next summit) the faint line of a path heading north toward the track. This is our way down.

First, we embark on a rough, steep descent, following a clearly trodden way zigzagging down the flank of **Cerro Verde** (NE), keeping an eye out for the occasional cairns.

Wp.8

Once on the saddle the path becomes less skittery. At the far end of the saddle, 650 metres from the trig point, just before the main path contours round the southern flank of the next rise (it eventually emerges at **Puerto Blanquillo**), we come to a large cairn, marking a minor path that descends to the left, passing to the right of an outcrop of rock (Wp.8 107M).

Turning left, we cross two dry run off gullies, then follow the path we saw from above, which joins the dirt track beside a small cairn (Wp.9 116M). We now simply turn left to enjoy easy downhill strolling and great views, ignoring a branch doubling back to the right (Wp.10 138M) before rejoining our outward route at the *fuente*, a little under four kilometres from Wp.9 (161M).

29

In this grand tour of a lovely valley, we take the popular path up **Arroyo Cueva del Melero** (the eponymous cave) and turn it into a circular walk using the dirt track on the northern flank of the valley. The climb to **Puerto Blanquillo** is a classic and the dirt track gives great views for negligible effort. That said, ten kilometres of dirt track won't be to everybody's taste, in which case treat it as a linear itinerary, possibly coupled with Walk 36. The climb crosses private land, but the wayposted rights of way are well established.

Access: see Walk 28

Heading upstream (Wp.1)

At the far end of the *área recreativa*, we ford **Arroyo Cueva del Melero**, then turn right and head upstream (Wp.1 0M). NB Ignore the waypost indicating the cobbled path on the nearside of the river. It lead to a bridge that has disappeared and it's easier to ford the river directly, though taking care as the rocks can be slippery.

Following the path along the right bank (our left) of the stream, we traverse long abandoned terraces amid dense vegetation, fording the stream again 370 metres upstream, after which we fork right at a Y-junction just short of a white water hut (Wp.2 6M).

After fording the stream twice more amid a dense tangle of oleander, our path climbs away from the watercourse and the valley widens above us, bringing **Cueva Melero** into view on our left. Opposite the cave, we cross cultivated terraces below **Cortijo Melero** then pass the farmhouse, accompanied by barking but friendly dogs.

From the *cortijo* entrance gates (Wp.3 21M), we follow the access track for a little over 100 metres until it doubles back to the right, at which point we carry straight on (NE) along a narrower track. The track brings us back to the riverbed, where it ends in a turning circle and we continue on a path, descending into the now dry riverbed.

500 metres later, we join another dirt track. 50 metres to the left, halfway through a steep, concrete S-bend, we turn left, as indicated by a cairn and, a few metres later, a waypost, recovering the old trail running parallel to the track (Wp.4 38M).

The trail rejoins the track at the top of the concrete 125 metres later. 75 metres up the track, which leads to **Cortijo Chaparral**, we fork right on a narrow path (Wp.5 43M), again marked with a cairn and a waypost, bringing into view the bright white rocks of **Puerto Blanquillo**.

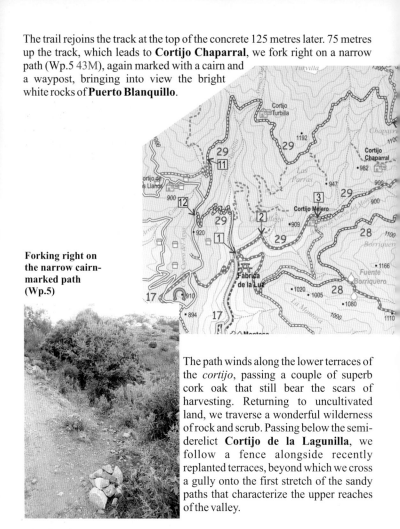

Forking right on the narrow cairn-marked path (Wp.5)

The path winds along the lower terraces of the *cortijo*, passing a couple of superb cork oak that still bear the scars of harvesting. Returning to uncultivated land, we traverse a wonderful wilderness of rock and scrub. Passing below the semi-derelict **Cortijo de la Lagunilla**, we follow a fence alongside recently replanted terraces, beyond which we cross a gully onto the first stretch of the sandy paths that characterize the upper reaches of the valley.

After crossing a rocky ridge, we drop back down to another coupling of waypost and cairn in the riverbed (Wp.6 65M). Following a rough way, invisible from below but revealing itself with every step, we climb along the watercourse, then cross another outcrop of rough rock before weaving through denser woodland. Beyond the wood, a final series of well-graded climbs end with a brief but steep climb onto the track from **Canillas** (Wp.7 82M).

A little under 300 metres to the left, at a sharp left hand bend on **Puerto Blanquillo**, we come to a confluence of trails, two on the right from **Cerro Verde** (Walk 28) and **Venta Cándido** (Walk 30) and directly ahead of us, the waypost route climbing NE to **Puerto de Cómpeta** (Wp.8 86M). Unless you're doing the linear route to Lucero (Walk 36), turn left here for the long trek along the dirt track round the northern flank of the valley.

After one and a half kilometres of easy walking during which we can really stretch our legs out, we ignore a track forking left for 'El Castaño' (Wp.9 102M).

Staying on the main track, we pass **Fuente La Teja** which is usually flowing.

Fuente la Teja

After crossing two more springs, the track climbs slightly to a junction with a branch on the right (Wp.10 127M).

The junction at Wp.10

We fork left on the main track, following a contour then descending gently (superb views opening out behind us toward **Lucero** and, up to the right, toward the eccentrically named **Malascamas** or Bad Beds), passing below a byre to reach a Y-junction (Wp.11 177M).

Views to Lucero

Forking left, we descend towards the south, then double back to the left at a junction 700 metres later (Wp.12 184M) for a final steep descent back to our starting point.

30 CÓMPETA: SENDERO CASA DE LA MINA & LOS PRADILLOS

A popular circuit featuring what is probably the finest path in the park and views second to none. En route we pass three deserted *ventas*, the old mule-skinners' taverns that were still operational in the late 1940s, serving the needs of the muleteers who would load up with fresh fish on the coast in the evening then cross the mountains and be in Granada by daybreak. Yes, quite. One old boy from **Frigiliana** is cited in David Baird's 'Between Two Fires' saying how his dad, one of the swiftest muleteers, used to complain that he had broken himself and 18 donkeys in the course of his career!

Access: on foot from Cómpeta

If arriving by car, from the **Venta de Palma** intersection above **Cómpeta**, just west of km4 on the A-7207 (the **Torrox** road), take the **Carril de Circunvalación** to the north, signposted 'Sendero Casa de la Mina/Pradillos' and 'Camp de Fútbol'. Fork right after 1200 metres on the steep lane climbing to the football ground 600 metres later (Wp.1). There's plenty of parking beside the main gate, always presuming there's not a match on, in which case you may have to park before the 1200 metre junction.

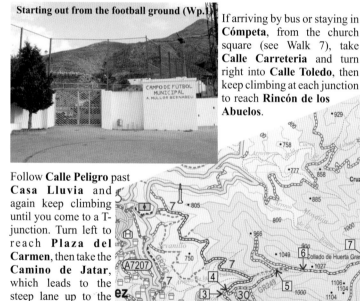

Starting out from the football ground (Wp.1)

If arriving by bus or staying in **Cómpeta**, from the church square (see Walk 7), take **Calle Carreteria** and turn right into **Calle Toledo**, then keep climbing at each junction to reach **Rincón de los Abuelos**.

Follow **Calle Peligro** past **Casa Lluvia** and again keep climbing until you come to a T-junction. Turn left to reach **Plaza del Carmen**, then take the **Camino de Jatar**, which leads to the steep lane up to the football ground.

From the football ground gates (Wp.1 0M), we climb a rough path to the right of the stadium (NE) leading to a spur track and a T-junction, where we turn left on the **GR249** (Wp.2 4M).

We now follow the clearly wayposted GR for seven kilometres to Wp.10, so after a preliminary read through, the book can be stowed.

Turning left at Wp.2

Climbing steadily on a stony track, we pass a cairn-marked route descending to the left (Wp.3 9M), 100 metres after which, we turn right at a junction of tracks (Wp.4 10M), continuing our steady ascent across the desiccated slopes behind **Cómpeta**. Ignoring two minor branches, we stick to the main track as it climbs alongside the **Arroyo de los Jurisdicciones** gully. When the track crosses the gully (Wp.5 23M), we turn right on a trail following the dry watercourse, rejoining the track 400 metres later (Wp.6 32M).

Carrying straight on, we traverse a stand of pine and a more pleasing prospect unfolds before us (there's not a lot to relieve the eye on the initial climb) over the lightly wooded slopes to the west of **Cerro Verde** (Walk 28) and **Cerro Atalaya** (the distinct rocky outcrop in the foreground), and beyond to the grand summit of **Lucero** (Walk 36).

900 metres later, we reach a wayposted junction on the **Collado de Huerta Grande** (Wp.7 44M).

From the far side of the *collado*, we can see the sea, the **Nerja** mountains, and (down below us) the blocky building of **Casa de la Mina**.

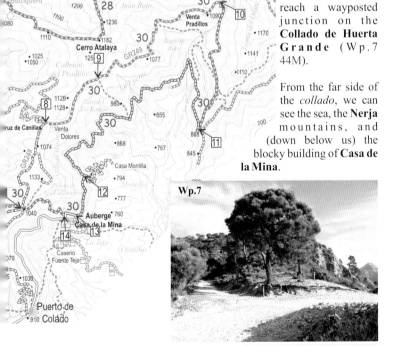
Wp.7

The yellow splashed cairn marks the head of the path we climb toward the end of the itinerary. For the present though, we bear left, as indicated by GR waypests, skirting behind **Peñón de los Calimacos**, which is topped by a firewatch hut and radio mast. We then descend to the **Collado Moyano**, beyond which we can see the ruins of the **Ventorillo Dolores**, also known as **Cortijo Maria Dolores**.

When the track veers left at a concrete bend on the *collado* (Wp.8 61M), we fork right on a broad trail passing in front of the *venta* which, even without Dolores to serve you a tot of brandy, is a beguiling spot for a break. We now follow a fabulous path, perhaps the finest in the park, heading toward **Lucero**, passing a narrow cairn-marked way descending to the right (Wp.9 76M) and two more ruined *ventas*, **Los Pradillos** (beyond which there is a fine threshing circle) and **Cándido**.

Our path at Wp.10

200 metres after the **Venta Cándido**, at a clearly sign and waypested junction, we leave the GR (which continues to **Frigiliana**) and the traditional donkey trail (which climbs to **Puerto Blanquillo**) (Wp.10 107M), and turn right on a slightly skittery path descending into the dry bed of **Arroyo de los Pradillos**.

Crossing the stream, we follow a clear path traversing the hillside through two gentle but relatively lengthy climbs. The path then runs alongside and crosses a firebreak before descending to join the dirt track (visible throughout most of the outward leg since Wp.8) between **Frigiliana** and **Cómpeta** (Wp.11 150M). We now simply turn right and follow this track for nearly five kilometres, all the way to **Casa de la Mina**, ignoring all branches, notably a major turning down to the left four kilometres later (Wp.12 189M).

Superb views after Wp.12

The walking is easy, the views superb. **Casa de la Mina** remains out of sight until the last moment, when we round a corner and reach a Y-junction between the *casa rural* and the former hotel (Wp.13 195M).

Forking right, we pass between the *casa rural* and hotel, ignoring a branch track descending to the left. 30 metres later, at a small electricity pylon, we double back to the right on a rough trail marked with cairns and waymarks (Wp.14 199M) that climbs to an overgrown platform, beyond which a clear path climbs steadily to rejoin our outward route at Wp.7 (216M).

31

El Fuerte was the last redoubt in the Axarquía of the sixteenth century Morisco rebellion and there are still some scant remains of the fortifications on the summit. Nowadays, the *cerro* is better known as a rather brilliant *mirador* offering commanding views across a large stretch of the sierra. If you're dependent on public transport and want one biggish climb, this very straightforward ascent is the one to do. Following a clear, well-maintained path with only one significant junction, it is also recommended for inexperienced walkers who want to test themselves on an energetic but simple itinerary.

Access: On foot from Frigiliana

By car, follow the bypass (*circunvalacion*) to the **Taller Los Cobos** roundabout and take the road out of the village. The walk starts 400 metres later on a concrete track signposted 'Sendero/Mirador/ Pozo de Lizar' (Wp.1). There's room to park alongside the road, at the bends 50 and 200 metres up the track, or (driving on dirt), beyond Wp.2, between the reservoir and the ruins of **Castillo Lizar**.

If arriving by bus, from **Plaza Ingenio** (Wp.Bus1), take the cobbled street climbing behind the playground into **Calle Real**, forking right at the Y junction onto a stairway street. Turn right 50 metres later for **Restaurante El Mirador** and **Panorámica**. Climbing at each junction, we pass in front of **Restaurante El Mirador** and carry straight on into a narrow alley, then turn right into **La Chorrera**. Forking left below house Nº12, we join a concrete lane that climbs steadily then levels off before coming to a T-junction (Wp.Bus2 13M). Turn right to reach the **Pozo de Lizar** reservoir 300 metres later (Wp.2).

The junction at our start (Wp.1)

From the 'Sendero / Mirador/Pozo de Lizar' junction (Wp.1 0M), we climb steadily along the track for 730 metres to a reservoir, the **Pozo de Lizar**, directly behind the knoll where the old castle used to stand (Wp.2 10M). On the nearside of the reservoir, we double back to the left on stairs climbing between a garage and a villa.

And that, basically, is all you need to know on this gloriously straightforward walk that, from this point on, doesn't really require any description at all.

Above the villa, we climb steadily to steeply, bringing the **Barranco de Higuerón** (Walk 11) into view. Rapidly gaining height in the pine forest behind **Frigiliana**, we pass in front of a first rocky outcrop on the ridge we follow to the foot of **El Fuerte**. Approaching a second rocky outcrop, we ignore a very minor way off to the right (Wp.3 41M). There's a second branch fifty metres later, but you probably won't notice it on the way up and, in any case, the two branches rejoin after fifty metres.

The ridge path

The junction at Wp.4

The trig point at Wp.5

Superb views open out toward **Lucero** (Walk 36) as we climb onto the back of the ridge before dropping back onto its southern flank again. After skirting countless rocky outcrops and crags overlooking the **Higuerón**, we reach a junction beside a solitary pine tree on a pass at the base of **El Fuerte** (Wp.4 77M).

Carrying straight on (W) along the main path, we climb to the summit, where there are some very vestigial vestiges of the **Morisco** fort and an equally dilapidated trig point (Wp.5 92M). We return the same way.

32

The climb to **Cerro Cruz del Pinto** is a popular walk and with good reason as it offers fabulous sea views and a superb perspective on the park's major summits, including **La Maroma** (Walk 35), **El Fuerte** (Walk 31), **Lucero** (Walk 36), and **Alto de Cielo** (Walk 38). It's relatively easy but gets a high exertion rating for the steep climb between Wps. 6 & 7. The summit is named for Francisco de Pinto, a sailor from Verona who got into a spot of bother in a storm off the Spanish coast in the sixteenth century and promised to raise a cross on the nearest summit if his ship made landfall.

4 | 2H 5M | 9.2 km | 350m / 350m | | 4

Access: see Walk 23

A 'brief encounter' at Wp.1

The start is the same as Walk 23, the first three waypoints of which appear in the waypoint file for the present itinerary. At the cement works (Wp.3 17M), we bear left on the surfaced track for 'Los Almáchares', the collective name for the *huertas*, *casetas*, *cortijos* and new villas above the confluence of the **Chillar** and **Higuerón** rivers.

Climbing steadily, we pass a rough track doubling back to the right toward the old quarry (Wp.4 25M). We stay on the surfaced track for a further 900 metres, ignoring branches accessing private property, and passing occasional signposts for 'Quinto Pino'.

Leaving the built up area, we reach a pinewood, where we briefly intersect with Walk 22 at a concrete branch climbing to the

103

right beside a 'Parque Natural' sign, signposted 'Quinto Pino' (Wp.5 37M). Turning right, we follow the concrete track for 200 metres until it swings left toward the gates of the **Quinto Pino** villa, the main way carrying straight on as a rough track.

Our narrow path at Wp.6

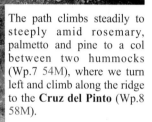

At this point, we turn right onto a narrow path flanked by cairns and marked by another 'Parque Natural' sign (Wp.6 41M).

Cruz del Pinto (Wp.8)

The path climbs steadily to steeply amid rosemary, palmetto and pine to a col between two hummocks (Wp.7 54M), where we turn left and climb along the ridge to the **Cruz del Pinto** (Wp.8 58M).

The descent to Wp.9

Behind the cross, a rough but less precipitous path descends to skirt to the right of a craggy, pine capped knoll, beyond which we rejoin Walk 22 at Wp.7 (Wp.9 62M).

Wp.9

Bearing left, we follow the track back round the base of **Cerro Cruz del Pinto** for a kilometre until it runs into the bend of another track above a small orchard (Wp.10 75M), where we carry straight on to rejoin our outward route at Wp.6 (79M).

At Wp.5, we can return the same way, or turn right to descend into the **Higuerón** (Wp.11 89M) and stroll downstream back to Wp.2 (113M).

33

Following an old dirt track on the outward leg and returning via the remarkable **Cerro Martos** path, this walk explores a wonderfully wild landscape of gorges and crags, visiting en route an exceptional natural phenomenon (and it really is phenomenal), the **Barranco de los Chortales** waterfalls, where logjams have been petrified by lime deposits. There is a slight but avoidable (see text) risk of vertigo above Wps. 5 & 6.

| 4 | 2H 35M | 9.2 km | | 400m / 400m | | | 0 |

Access: by car

Wp.1 is at km.31

Wp.1 is at km31 of the A-4050, signposted 'Jete' and 'Otivar' from the centre of **Almuñécar**. Immediately before the kilometre post, there's a large parking bay on the right.

Additional parking is available further south, 100 metres before the 'Rio Verde' mapboard. Note, this is the second 'Rio Verde' mapboard as you drive up from the south, 2.1km after the first. The first mapboard is where the non-vertiginous option joins the road (see text).

The second mapboard

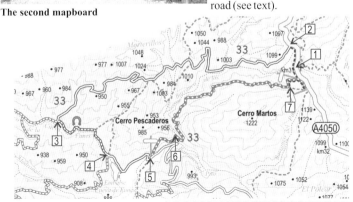

105

From km31 of the A-4050 (Wp.1 0M), we stroll along the road to the north for 250 metres, then turn left on a rough, eroded track blocked to traffic by a chain (Wp.2 3M). We follow this track for four-and-a-half kilometres. After a little over a kilometre of steady descent (our return path clearly visible as it snakes along the pinnacle stippled flank of **Cerro Martos** to the south), the track runs into the **Chortales** riverbed.

200 metres later, the track veers right and climbs into an affluent *barranco*, contouring round the watercourse before climbing to the first of two passes, the second visible to the west. After descending into a dell, we climb steadily to cross the second pass.

Traversing an ever wilder and more desiccated landscape of limestone, scrub and pine, we cross a firebreak below **Cerro Lopera** (Walk 14), then wind through a steep chicane onto a better maintained stretch of track that descends to a junction beside a cabin in a cave, the **Cueva de Funes** (Wp.3 60M).

Cueva de Funes

Turning left, we follow a well stabilized track to a junction behind the **Embalse de Cueva de Funes** reservoir (Wp.4 72M). Bearing left, we skirt the reservoir then descend into a spectacular hollow below the orange flecked cliffs of **Cerro Martos**. 500 metres after the reservoir, just above a concrete ford on the **Chortales** torrent, we join the wayposted 'Río Verde' route at a sharp left hand bend beside an information board about canyoning (Wp.5 85M).

Turning left, we take a narrow path on the inside of the bend, descending to cross the stream before climbing steeply to a slightly vertiginous traverse.

If you don't want to tackle this, stay on the track at Wp.5 for a couple of hundred metres until it doubles back to the right, where a path on the left leads to the waterfall.

If the steep climb after that doesn't appeal, follow the track back up to the road, two kilometres from our starting point.

The waterfall of petrified wood

Shortly after the vertiginous traverse, we reach the waterfall of petrified wood (Wp.6 96M).

I won't describe it, you really need to see it for yourself, and don't neglect to explore the cave behind the falls, accessed via a path a few metres further east.

Beyond the waterfall, at the junction with the cave path, four rough steps access a brief stretch of path leading to the steep flight of steps that climb onto **Cerro Martos**. These are well-made and fitted with balustrades, so only the most acutely sensitive vertigo sufferers should have any problem.

The cave behind the falls

After the first steep climb, the path (rather disappointingly) drops down below a pinnacle of rock then climbs over rough rock and embarks upon its extraordinarily serpentine progress along the northern flank of **Cerro Martos**, climbing steadily, then gently, then steadily again. The final stretch dips up and down on varying gradients before passing a turning on the right (Wp.7 147M) 300 metres from our starting point.

Top of the world stuff, **Torrecilla** is the **Great Western Mirador**, a mini-**Maroma** with all of the appeal of Walk 35 but not nearly so daunting. Despite or perhaps because of its simplicity, this is a deeply satisfying outing, a big uncomplicated climb with great views for those who want to stretch a leg and breath deep without fussing about pathfinding or orientation. Global times and distances include the optional loop via the old path at the end. *Plan on being out for about five hours including breaks.*

Access: (by car)
Arriving in **Alcaucín** via the MA-4104, immediately after the green ceramic sign at the entrance to the conurbation ('Alcaucín / Paraiso Natural / Bienvenidos'), take the paved lane on the left, signposted '**Área Recreativa Cortijo del Alcázar**', setting the odometer at zero. Fork right at km 1.4. After two kilometres, we pass the '**Albergues de Carrión** Bungalows' branch on our right and the tarmac ends. You can park here, but the remaining track to the start is only 400 metres and 200 of that is on concrete, the rest smoother than many Spanish roads, so you'd really have to be tender toward your car hirer to shy away from this one! Park at the lay-by at km2.5.

The walk starts just after the bend beyond the parking bay on a chained-off track (concreted for the first 100 metres) doubling back to the right and climbing past a sign prohibiting unauthorized motorized traffic (Wp.1 0M).

Climbing steadily to steeply, we reach a sharp, right-hand bend 830 metres later, within

The chained track marking our start

sight of the western end of **Maroma** and overlooking the **Alcázar** *área recreativa* (Wp.2 12M). On the cusp of the bend there is a junction with a stretch of the old path that was obliterated by the dirt track. We can take this now or, in the spirit of the itinerary (Easy Walking - Grand Vistas) stick with the track, heading southwest, views opening out over the cultivated plains of western Axarquía, views that improve exponentially as we pass a second concrete bend, from where we can see the **Viñuela** dam and, high above us, the flank of **Torrecilla**.

The old path and new track rejoin at another sharp right hand bend (Wp.3 36M), 500 metres after which, we pass a path branching off to the right (Wp.4 49M). After nearly 4.5km of steady trudging, we reach a Y-junction (Wp.5 64M) where we fork right to continue climbing, superb views opening out over the dramatic crags behind the **Alcázar** *área recreativa*.

Dramatic crags behind Alcázar

A final steep climb brings us to the end of the dirt track, 50 metres beyond which (Wp.6 74M) a rough way zigzags up to a T-junction with a clear path climbing from the village (Wp.7 76M).

Turning left, we follow the zigzagging path up to the summit crest, though a word to the wise, the high point of this walk is one of those devious little blighters that keeps tucking itself behind what you think must be the top.

To complete the **Maroma** analogy, we even pass a small sinkhole (Wp.8 102M) 300 metres before reaching the cairn-capped crest that is the culminating point of our itinerary (Wp.9 105M).

Wonderful views from the top

We return the same way with the option of taking the old path at Wp.3, a slightly shorter and more attractive option, shadier and softer under foot, though you do have to clamber over several fallen trees. Don't be alarmed when it climbs briefly. It does soon start to descend.

35 CANILLAS DE ACEITUNO: LA MAROMA

This is The Big One, the highest summit in the **Sierra Tejeda**, the westernmost 2000 metre summit on the Iberian Peninsula, the biggest climb in the book, and an ascent that many Malagueños regard as a patriotic pilgrimage. The **Sendero Casa de la Nieve**, the old snow gatherers' path from **Canillas de Aceituno**, is a hell of a climb and not for the faint of heart (not for the faint of anything come to that), but if you're up for it, it's a walk you won't forget. Once out of the village, the route is clear, and on the whole well marked with waypoints and cairns. However, the last stretch is off path and should not be attempted when visibility is poor.

5   6H *   19.6 km   1321m   **out & back**   1321m   2

*Including breaks, allow at least 4½ hours for the ascent and 3½ hours for the descent.

Access: see Walk 27

The start is the same as Walk 27, the first nine waypoints of which are included in the waypoint file for the present itinerary. At the **Collado de los Charcones** Y-junction (Wp.9 109M), we leave Walk 27 and take

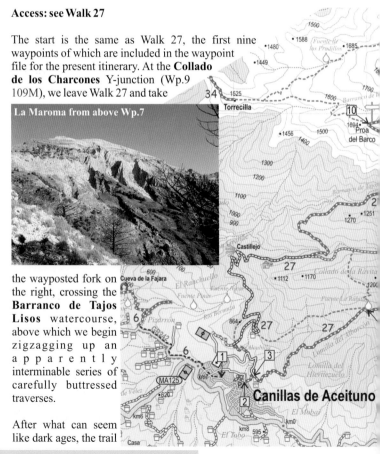

La Maroma from above Wp.7

the waypoted fork on the right, crossing the **Barranco de Tajos Lisos** watercourse, above which we begin zigzagging up an apparently interminable series of carefully buttressed traverses.

After what can seem like dark ages, the trail

Our junction at Wp.9

passes a waypost on a splendid little promontory, the evocatively named **Proa del Barco** (Prow of the Boat), which overlooks **Barranco de la Cueva de Don Pedro** (Wp.10 144M). We have a climb of nearly 400 metres ahead of us!

Views from below Wp.10

Veering right (ENE), we continue climbing on a rockier path, following cairns, the occasional waypost, and old green waymarks along the flank of the **Cueva de Don Pedro** gully, toward the head

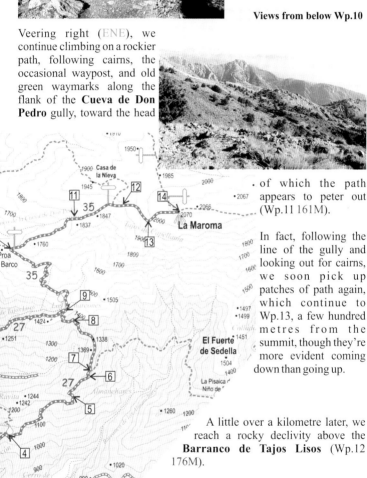

of which the path appears to peter out (Wp.11 161M).

In fact, following the line of the gully and looking out for cairns, we soon pick up patches of path again, which continue to Wp.13, a few hundred metres from the summit, though they're more evident coming down than going up.

A little over a kilometre later, we reach a rocky declivity above the **Barranco de Tajos Lisos** (Wp.12 176M).

Looking up to the left here, you should be able to pick out the low walls of a ruin 200 metres away and, more easily discernible, a yellow plaque. This is the eponymous **Casa de la Nieve**, where snow used to be packed down in winter for medicinal and culinary use in the summer.

To reach the summit, we carry straight on (E), embarking on our final steep climb, picking our way from cairn to cairn and favouring the southern flank of the rise, following an easing gradient heading towards a large cairn silhouetted against the horizon.

The pathless ascent after Wp.13

From the cairn (Wp.13 187M), we veer left, now within sight of the summit, following a broad thoroughfare of cairn-marked ways (NE).

The trig point is invisible until the last fifty metres, but off to the right there is a fence enclosing the largest of the summit's sinkholes. The trig point (Wp.14 197M) lies behind and to the left of this sinkhole. If your breath hasn't been taken already, the views should do the job. We return via the same route.

The trig point

36

Dominating the skyline east of **Málaga**, the triangular peak of **Lucero** or **Raspón de los Moriscos** can stake a strong claim to being the *Parque Natural*'s emblematic mountain, irresistibly drawing the eye skyward and uplifting the heart in a similar manner when you're standing on the summit. It's one of the wildest and most dramatic peaks in the area, with views to match. In short, essential walking. There is a *risk of vertigo* on the final 300 metres.

The dirt track to **Puerto Blanquillo** is very long. If you don't want to drive it, use Walk 29 Wps.1 to 8 to reach **Puerto Blanquillo**. We have prepared two waypoint files for this itinerary, one starting at **Fábrica de la Luz**, the other from **Puerto Blanquillo**.

If you intend driving and want to check the track in advance, do Walk 28 first. It's also worthwhile asking **Cómpeta** or **Canillas** tourism offices about the state of the track. If there's a strong wind at **Puerto Blanquillo** (which there often is) turn back. What's strong at the *puerto* will be even stronger on the summit. Allow five hours if doing the walk from **Puerto Blanquillo**, eight from **Fábrica de la Luz**.

From Fábrica de la Luz

From Puerto Blanquillo

Access:
To reach **Puerto Blanquillo** by car, set the odometer at 0 at the **Santa Ana** chapel in **Canillas** and take the 'Fábrica de la Luz' lane. Fork right at km1.2, leaving the *fábrica* lane. At the sharp right-hand bend at km1.9, leave the surfaced road and carry straight on along the dirt track. Ignore branches doubling back to the right at km4, and descending to the left at km5.6 and km8.7. **Puerto Blanquillo** is the sharp left-hand bend at km11.7. The drive takes the best part of an hour in a heavy camper van, but is considerably quicker in a lighter vehicle.

The bright white path at Wp.1

It is not recommended for low slung vehicles. There is ample room for parking along the track either side of **Puerto Blanquillo**.

From **Puerto Blanquillo**, we take the bright white wayposted path climbing above the track (NE) (Wp.8/1 0M).

Carrying straight on along the main wayposted trail at a junction with a cairn marked path doubling back to the right (Wp.9/2 8M), we stroll along a balcony path before climbing slightly to cross a gully and enter a hanger of pine trees. 50 metres into the woods, we come to a crossroads where a rough trail marked by a couple of cairns climbs to the right, (Wp.10/3 11M).

Sierra Nevada seen from Puerto de Cómpeta

Turning right, we leave the tree cover and climb to the **Puerto de Cómpeta** pass (Wp.11/4 22M) where superb views open out, first toward the **Sierra Nevada** then across the old marble quarry to the ragged back of **Lucero**. Descending gently on the far side of the pass, we join the quarry access track beside a cluster of derelict buildings.

Raspón de los Moriscos path (Wp.13/6)

200 metres later, at a junction with another track climbing to the left (Wp.12/5 26M), we bear right to descend past the **Fuente Barrera** fire fighting reservoir, from where we can already see the pinprick block of the old civil guard post on top of **Lucero**.

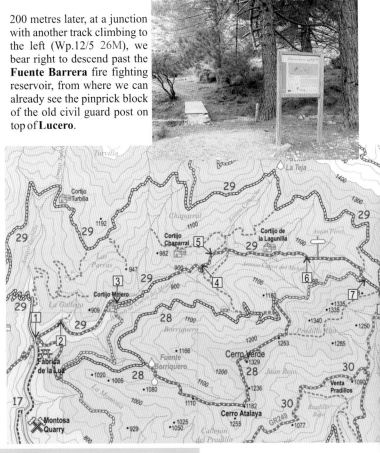

500 metres later, a mapboard, waypost and footbridge indicate the start of the 'Raspón de los Moriscos' path (Wp.13/6 34M).

Crossing the footbridge, we climb gently (E), bringing the **Sierra Nevada** back into view before the path curves into a more southerly orientation, climbing more steadily. On a broad shoulder below **Cerro de Rajas Negras**, we pass a waypost (Wp.14/7 59M) in front of the imposing little summit of **Cerro de la Mota**.

After a very brief descent, we resume our stony climb, crossing two small rises, from the first of which we see the main summit again, looking considerably more daunting than it did from lower down. Descending from the second rise, we cross **Collado de la Perdiz**, a broad pass within sight of the sea, where a couple of pathless routes join our itinerary.

Lucero, seem from above Perdiz

Sticking to the main trail, we pass a small 'MP' boundary marker for Málaga Province (Wp.15/8 79M), bringing into clearer relief the final zigzagging path to the top.

Ignoring a couple of shortcuts, we climb toward **Lucero**'s smaller sibling, **Lucerillo** (little bright star).

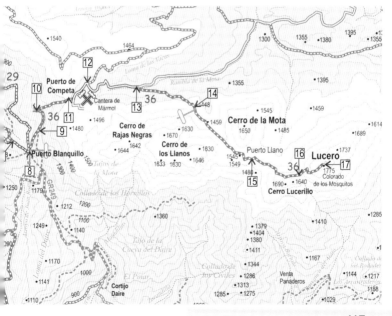

The traverse behind Lucerillo

A little way below the summit of **Lucerillo**, the gradient levels off for an easterly traverse to the tiny col between the two summits, **Coladero de los Mosquitos** (Wp.16/9 94M).

If things seem a bit too airy for your tastes at this stage, turn back now, as it gets considerably airier on the final climb and even more so on the way back down. Otherwise, we simply slog our way up the final, tightening zigzags to the peak of **Lucero** (Wp.17/10 109M).

We return by the same path, taking particular care on the more exposed bends at the beginning.

37

A classic among classics, the itinerary that has long defined walking in the region, the **Limán Trail** between **Frigiliana** and the **Cuevas de Nerja** is a grand little rollercoaster taking us into really remote terrain with great views over the **Río Chillar**.

The walk has always been well waymarked, but since its incorporation into the **GR249**, description is all but superfluous. The only moment you will need to consult the book en route is crossing the **Chillar** (Wps.7-8). Plan on being out for 5 – 6 hours.

If you intend eating at the **Fuente del Esparto** *albergue*, best check in advance that they are open (T. 678 771 281 / 951 197 501).

5   (3H 20M)   14 km   655m / 930m   one way   5

Access: see Walk 10

The start is the same as Walk 10, the first three waypoints of which are included in the waypoint file for the present itinerary.

75 metres after the **Pozo Batán** reservoir, we turn right on the GR signposted path leaving the riverbed (Wp.3 17M); see photo on the next page.

Climbing steadily to steeply, we zigzag up to a rocky col below **Cerro Felix** (Walk 22) (Wp.4 34M), where we carry straight on (NE), views opening out over a landscape that rapidly lends legitimacy to the rollercoaster analogy.

The path leaving the riverbed (Wp.3)

There's no call to be consulting a book or anything else apart from your senses up here and all you really need to know is that we fork right at the Y-junction 350 metres later (Wp.5 40M) to embark on our rollering and our coastering.

To give you an idea of what to expect, our path snakes its way along the dry slopes of the **Loma de Garza**, passing an off path route that descends a gully on the right (Wp.6 47M). We then climb a small rise, beyond which superb views open out over the **Chillar** valley and the mountains towering over its headwaters. The rollercoaster really kicks in now as the path dips in and out of the convolute folds feeding the **Chillar**.

Descent to the Chillar

Toward the end of the folds, intermittent cobbling leads us into a dry watercourse, which we follow for 75 metres before a steady, zigzagging, 100 metre ascent brings us onto the ridge above **Cuesta de Jiménez**, overlooking the main **Chillar** watercourse, beyond which we can see the horizontal line of an *acequia* and the fainter zigzags of our ongoing path.

We now descend to the wonderful wild, upper reaches of the **Chillar**, a superbly isolated spot despite the popularity of this itinerary and the proximity of **Nerja**.

Plunge pool in the river bed

Just above the river, we ignore a branch to the left (Wp.7 93M) and descend to the riverbed for a break and a bathe before our second big climb of the day, up to the **Collado de los Galgos** dirt track.

This is the only point at which you may need to consult the book as the river crossing isn't obvious. We don't ford it immediately, but descend alongside the right bank, following the waymarks to reach a ford above a mini waterfall 75 metres downstream (Wp.8 98M).

Once across the river, we bear right, slithering over a large boulder to continue along the left bank, where the route is confirmed by a waypost and waymarks.

Ford above a mini waterfall (Wp.8)

Following an increasingly clear path, we climb steeply to cross the *acequia* we saw earlier (considerably higher up the flank of the valley than it looked from the far side) (Wp.9 106M).

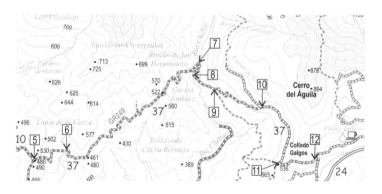

We now embark on a steady climb, briefly interrupted by a couple of short dips. After the initial haul the gradient eases and the path traces out a winding ascent, before finally joining a dirt track (Wp.10 127M). At this point we are a little over halfway through the walk. The remaining route is on good dirt tracks apart from one brief stretch on a rough trail.

Turning right, we follow the track to the **Collado de los Galgos** pass on the **Apretaderos** ridge (Wp.11 137M). Ignoring the path and trail that continue along the back of the ridge, we stay on the track as it descends (E) toward the **Pinarillo** *área recreativa*.

400 metres later, we reach a junction where an old track (now reduced to an eroded trail) forks right (Wp.12 142M).

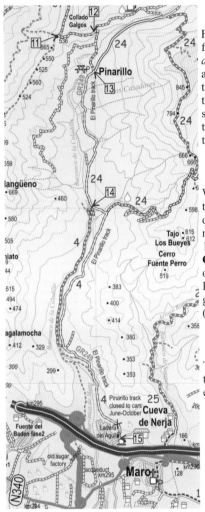

For refreshment, carry straight on for the **Fuente del Esparto** *albergue*. Otherwise, fork right and follow the eroded trail into the **Pinarillo** *área recreativa*, on the far side of which, in front of a small kiosk (Wp.13 148M), we turn right on the main access track.

We follow this track all the way to the **Cuevas de Nerja**, with the option of forking right 1600 metres after the kiosk (Wp.14 165M) into **Barranco de Coladilla**, doing the outward leg of Walk 4 (Wps.1-4) in reverse. Either way, the track ends at the gates of the **Cuevas de Nerja** (Wp.21 200M).

The bus stop is in the car park on the left. There are buses to **Nerja** every 30 to 60 minutes.

38

Alto de Cielo, as seen on the approach

The highest mountain on the Iberian littoral (defined as within 6km of the sea), **Alto de Cielo** is the **Sierra de Almijara**'s most popular *mirador*, offering great views over the coast, the major peaks in the hinterland, the snowy heights of **Sierra Nevada**, and occasionally even North Africa.

The linear ascent via **Cortijo de la Civila** is clearly marked with wayposts and cairns, and can be followed without consulting the book en route. It is not recommended in hot weather or when visibility is poor. For access by bus and to avoid dirt track driving, see Walks 4 & 25.

5 | 4H 10M | * | 14.6 km | 1170m 1170m | out & back | 0

*You should allow at least six hours including breaks.**

Access: (by car), see Walk 24

Taking the 'Sendero' track (Wp.1 0M), we climb steadily for 375 metres to a concrete bend, where we reach the first of three clearly wayposted shortcuts avoiding a series of chicanes in the dirt track. At the top of the third shortcut

Taking the 'Sendero' at Wp.1

The junction at Wp.4

(Wp.2 16M), we turn left. After a steady slog, the track levels off briefly to cross a cutting, beyond which we ignore paths branching left and right (Wp.3 29M). Sticking with the track, we descend slightly to cross **Arroyo Romero**.

Climbing steadily again, almost always within sight of the summit, we pass the ruins of **Cortijo de la Civila**, 125 metres after which we reach a junction below a second abandoned building of more recent construction (Wp.4 52M).

Bearing left, we can take either of the trails round the abandoned building, behind which they merge in a broad trail climbing (N) to an information panel about *cabras montés*, where the trail veers right and dwindles to a rocky but clearly defined path.

... views open out to the east ...

A steady ascent, during which the path is never in doubt and is in any case confirmed by a superfluity of wayposts, takes us through the last scattered pine up to the tip of a long spur, where views open out to the east (Wp.5 88M). Bearing left, we continue to climb (N) toward the bulbous summit rocks, following a clear path with patches of natural paving.

Forking left when the path splits for a couple of hundred metres (Wp.6 97M), we contour to the left of a large cone of rock below the main summit.

Beyond the cone, a solitary pine offers one of the last patches of shade before we cross a saddle clad in oak scrub to embark on the last and steepest 200 metres of our climb, following a rough path patched with scree.

Traversing the western flank of the summit rocks, which are considerably more ragged and less monolithic from this perspective, we climb steeply across cairn studded rock, bringing into view the mirrored cross on the summit 80 metres above us.

50 metres below the summit, an off-path route feeds in from the left (take care not to stray onto this when descending) (Wp.7 129M), soon after which we reach the trig point (Wp.8 135M), tucked behind the summit cross, which is said to have been erected by a shipwrecked German sailor in the seventeenth century.

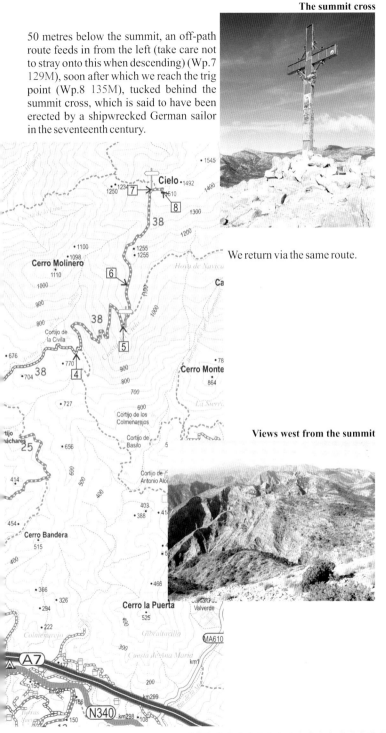

We return via the same route.

Views west from the summit

APPENDICES

Please note:
Telephone numbers are shown in red. When dialling from outside Axarquía, prefix these numbers with 00 34. Websites and email addresses are shown in green.

A USEFUL INFORMATION

TAXIS
There are a number of local taxi services, including:

Taxi Frigiliana	696 96 94 69
Taxi Torre del Mar	659 15 50 54
Taxi Vélez-Málaga	622 02 20 40
Máximo Fernández, Cómpeta	657 50 69 54
Taxi Nerja	952 52 05 37

Accommodation: Casas Rurales

If you would prefer to stay in a small hotel or guest-house, away from mass tourism, try the following:

www.allrural.com
www.antiquanatura.com
www.clubrural.com
www.masrural.com
www.toprural.com

MISCELLANEOUS INFORMATION

Bus Information

https://www.alsa.es/en/

Background Information

www.andalucia.com
http://www.malaga.es/en/turismo/
http://www.visitcostadelsol.com/
www.tourspain.es
www.spain-info.com
www.visitacostadelsol.com

Phone Numbers

Emergency (police, ambulance, fire brigade)	112
Medical emergencies	061
Guardia Civil	062
Local Police	092
National Police	091
Fire Brigade	080
Sea Rescue	900 202 202

There's enough variety in Walk! Costa del Sol (Axarquía) to cater for most tastes, from holidaymakers wanting a day away from the beach to the serious hiker on a dedicated walking trip. However, there is no such thing as a fully comprehensive guide to an area like this, not one you can lift off the floor at least, and there are plenty of other excursions and ways into these mountains. Hyperlinks to the sites mentioned below will be posted on the Facebook page.

https://www.facebook.com/WalkCostadelSolAxarquia

Guided Walking

There are several guided walking companies operating in the region and these are worth considering if you want to do a bit of peak bagging without the big climbs entailed by our policy of avoiding driving on dirt tracks. Two classic examples of off-road approaches used by guided walk companies are climbing **La Maroma** from the **Llanos de Sedella** and **Lucero** from **Cortijo Daire**.

We were greatly assisted in the preparation of this book by Joost Schepel, a Dutch guide who speaks perfect English and operates out of **Cómpeta** with his son, Duncan. They offer a wide range of guided day walks, guided and self-guided packages, and stage a walking festival in September. Their services are highly recommended.

Contact them directly by phone:

Tel: (34) 619 511 104 or check out their website: www.walkspain.co.uk/

Other local companies offering similar services are:

AndalucianWalks   www.andalucianwalks.com/

Holiday Nerja   www.holidaynerja.co.uk/guided_walks_in_nerja.htm

John Keo Walking Tours   www.hikingwalkingspain.com/

Salamandra   www.malaga-aventura.es/senderismo.php

Packages

Package holidays for walkers in the region are available through:

Spanish Highs   www.spanishhighs.co.uk

World Walks   https://worldwalks.com/

Wow Walks   www.wow247.co.uk

More Walking Ideas

Obviously, the Internet is a good source of ideas, though it should be treated with caution, in particular routes posted on GPS file sharing sites like Wikiloc. If you know the terrain, these can be useful, but such sites tend to bring out the gung-ho, "Look what I can do" tendencies in certain walkers, and you may find yourself embarking on an adventure that is, well, absolutely barking.

More reliable (because they are more prudent in their recommendations) are the tourism office sites, the best of which is the **Frigiliana** site:

www.turismofrigiliana.es/rutas-de-senderismo.html

Most of their itineraries feature in our own walks, but there are some alternatives.

The **Cómpeta** site is in Spanish, but links to a site offering GPS data:

www.compiteando.es/index.php/tracks-gps

The **Nerja** site: www.nerja.es/

- proposes six itineraries, four of which appear in the present publication. We did not include the **Navachica** and **Peñon de los Castillejos** itineraries, as the former has been cut by erosion and the latter marred by fly-tipping.

Decent leaflets about walks beginning in their respective municipalities are produced by the local authorities in **Frigiliana**, **Canillas de Aceituno** and **Sayalonga**. These are available in digital form from the **Frigiliana** site and from the following two sites, though the first is only in Spanish:

www.canillasdeaceituno.es/es/Sobre_Canillas/Rutas_de_Senderismo/

http://fr.calameo.com/read/0006038358d1a827a4220

Cómpeta Tourism Office offers multilingual leaflets describing official itineraries around the village, but given less than perfect translations and sketchy maps, these are not great value for money at one euro a walk.

Rather better value is the ambitious programme of guided walks run by **Almuñécar** town hall. They charge 12 euros a head, but it's worth it for the bus drop off/pick up at either end, often in places where there is no other bus service. Details are available in **Almuñécar Tourism Office**.

Blogs

There are numerous individuals blogging about walking in the area, mainly in Spanish, but there are three decent English language sites:

www.axarquiaonfoot.com/

www.larswalking.com/walks/

www.travelpod.com/travel-blog/mrvince1952/1/tpod.html

Long Distance Walk

If you want to do a long distance walk, a large part of the GR249 *Gran Senda de Málaga* (a 650km tour of the entire province) features on the map. You can download details and GPS tracks for the various stages by clicking on the interactive map at:

www.gransendademalaga.es/en/

The complete GPS track file can be downloaded at:

www.gpsies.com

The coastal sections are not recommended, but apart from one unconscionably long stretch of tarmac, the mountain sections feature some very fine paths indeed.

Further Afield

If your stay is prolonged or you are a repeat visitor, it's worth venturing further afield to explore the **Sierras de Tejeda** and **Almijara** from the north, approaches that are covered by the Tour and Trail map. The ascents of **La Maroma** from the **Alcázar** *área recreativa* above **Alcaucín** or the **Sendero el Robledal** near the **Cortijo el Cerezal** *zona de acampada* (details on the Facebook page) are classics.

A popular family day out is to explore the river pools at **La Resinera** near **Fornes** on the approach to more river-splashing fun in the **Río Cebollón** (reputedly the cleanest river in the region) and **Barranco Bacal**, also covered by the map and featured as extras on the Facebook page:

https://www.facebook.com/WalkCostadelSolAxarquia/

C PUBLICATIONS

Maps

Costa del Sol (Axarquia Tour & Trail Super-Durable Map (published by Discovery Walking Guides) is, naturally, the best.

Penibetica produce a map at the same scale, but it's a bit cluttered and some itineraries are risky.

If you want extra detail, some years ago, a local engineer, Miguel Angel Torres Delgado, produced two very detailed and very old-fashioned looking OS-style 1:25,000 maps of the **Sierras de Tejeda** and **Almijara**, which have been repackaged in a booklet available in local bookshops.

Walking Books

I haven't used any of the following publications, but a glance at the contents suggests *The Mountains of Nerja: Sierras Tejeda, Almijara Y Alhama* Paperback – 15 Sep 2014 (ISBN: 978185284754) by Jim Ryan could be useful for additional high summits.

The car tours in **Andalucia: Costa del Sol and Sierras** (Landscapes) Paperback – 4 Jun 2015 (9781856914727) by John and Christine Oldfield would supplement exploring with the Tour and Trail Map.

The *Rother* guide spreads itself rather thin, including as it does the Costa del Sol, the Costa del Luz, AND the Sierra Nevada in a single volume.

Long term resident in Andalusia and walking guide Guy Hunter-Watts: www.guyhunterwatts.com/ has also published several books about the region.

Background Reading

East of Málaga - Essential Guide to the Axarquía and Costa Tropical Paperback - 31 Mar 2015 (ISBN: 9788460663416) Author: David Baird

Handy information guide including what to see, where to stay, food and drink, local history etc.

Andalucia: A Literary Guide for Travellers Hardcover - 23 Sep 2016 Authors: Andrew and Suzanne Edwards (ISBN: 9781784533908)

Andalucia as seen through the eyes and words of a host of authors and poets over several centuries.

Wild Flowers of Eastern Andalucia: A Field Guide to the Flowering Plants of Almeria and the Sierra De Los Filabres Region Paperback – 7 Mar 2014 (ISBN: 9780956396112) Author: Sarah Ball

Well organised illustrated guide.

A Selection of Wildflowers of Southern Spain Paperback - 31 Jul 2000 (ISBN: 9788489954120)

Over 200 commonly spotted wildflowers from coast to mountains, illustrated.

Where to Watch Birds in Southern and Western Spain: Andalucaia, Extremadura and Gibraltar (Where to Watch Birds) Paperback – 25 Mar 2008 (ISBN 9780713683158) Authors: Andrew Paterson, Ernest Garcia

Though the book covers a wide area, there are relevant sections for Andalucía.Be aware that development may have affected some suggested locations.

Traditional Recipes of the Axarquía Paperback - 1 Jun 2013 (9788494085369) Author: Malcolm Coxall

As well as recipes, there's a short introduction to the area's history and geography, and how this has influenced local produce and cuisine.

Bike Hire

A quick internet search will reveal several companies that hire bikes, either for self-guided cyclists or with the option of cycling in a group with an experienced leader.

Amongst others, for guided cycle rides try:

http://www.malaga-aventura.es/multi-adventure/bike-rides.php

Bike2Malaga is a useful resource for bikers in the Malaga area. They rent bikes, offer delivery and pickup services and have detailed bike routes on their website. Cycle with a guide or go self-guided. There are a number of cycling routes available via links from their website; those selected cycling routes (below) can be found on:

www.bike2malaga.com/en

Cycling Routes

Málaga - Casabermeja - Colmenar - Riogordo - Periana - Viñuela - Vélez-Málaga - Torre del Mar - Málaga

level 4 | 113 km, circular
Climbs & Descents: 1957 m

Download this trail to your GPS, Google Earth or Open Map from Wikiloc:

https://tinyurl.com/y7ytzccg

Málaga - Puerto del Leon - Santopitar - Comares - Vélez-Málaga - Torre del Mar - Málaga

level 4 | 98 km, circular
Climbs & Descents: 1995 m

Download this trail to your GPS, Google Earth or Open Map from Wikiloc:

https://tinyurl.com/y84aeubz

Málaga - Torre del Mar - Vélez-Málaga - Benamocarra - Iznate - Cajiz - Benajarafe - Málaga

level 2 | 80 km, circular
Climbs & Descents: 621 m

Download this trail to your GPS, Google Earth or Open Map from Wikiloc:

https://tinyurl.com/yaylm3w6

Málaga - Colmenar - Riogordo - Periana - Viñuela - Torre del Mar - Rincón de la Victoria - Málaga

level 4 | 112 km, circular
Climbs & Descents: 1810 m

Download this trail to your GPS, Google Earth or Open Map from Wikiloc:

https://tinyurl.com/y833ltp6

We Welcome Your Feedback

Discovery Walking Guides is a business, but it's also a passion for us. Really we are a 'Happiness' organisation hoping to bring you happiness through using the outdoor adventures in our 'Walk!' books and 'Tour & Trail' maps. Our objective is to give you reliable, re-creatable walking adventures that you can enjoy. Your happiness is our happiness.

You are our most valuable resource for keeping us up to date with how our books and maps are performing. We want to hear from you; praise is always welcome but some of our best improvements have come from criticism. Criticism can be hard to take, but we recognise that your observations and opinions are valuable if we are to produce better books and maps in the future.

If you discover that things have changed since a 'Walk!' book or 'Tour & Trail' map was published let us know. If you think we could do things better, please let us know.

We receive a lot of emails from our DWG 'family', all of them valuable and all of them replied to as soon as possible.
Send us your updates, praise, criticism and ideas at:

ask.discovery@ntlworld.com

Costa del Sol (Axarquía) Tour & Trail Super-Durable Map

We recommend Costa del Sol (Axarquía) Tour & Trail Super-Durable Map to complement this guidebook.

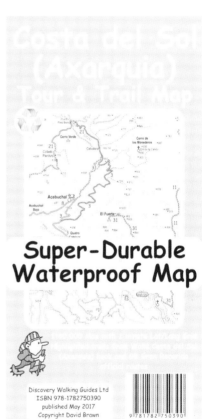

- 1:40,000 scale map

- 1 minute Lat/Long grid

- highlighted trails from Walk! Costa del Sol (Axarquía) guidebook

- GR (Gran Recorrido) official routes

- waterproof

- virtually tear-proof

- map guaranteed for 2 years of adventurous use

- printed on recyclable polyart (high-density polyethylene)

- digital Costa del Sol (Axarquía) Tour & Trail Map is available as a free download from the Discovery Walking Guides website:

www.dwgwalking.co.uk

Super-Durable Waterproof Map

Discovery Walking Guides Ltd
ISBN 978-1782750390
published May 2017
Copyright David Brawn

GLOSSARY

This glossary contains Spanish and Canarian words found in the text (shown in *italics*) plus other local words that you may encounter.

a

abandonado	abandoned, in poor repair
abierto	open
acampamiento	camping
acantilado	cliff
acequia	water channel
agua	water
agua no potable	water (not drinkable)
agua potable	drinking water
alto	high
aparcamiento	parking
área recreativa	designated picnic spot; may have tables, water supply
arroyo	stream
autopista	main road, motorway
ayuntamiento	town hall

b

bajo	low
barranco	ravine
bocadillo	bread roll
bodegón	inn
bosque	wood

c

cabezo	peak, summit
cabra montés	mountain goat
calle	street
camino	trail, path, track
camino particular	private road
camino real	old donkey trail (lit. royal road)
carretera	main road
casa	house
casa rural	country house accommodation to let
cascada	waterfall
caserío	hamlet, village
cementario	cemetry
cerrado	closed
cerro	hill, mountain without a real peak
cerveza	beer
choza	shelter
clinica	clinic, hospital
colmena	bee hive
comida	food
cordillera	mountain range
correos	post office
cortijo	farmstead
costa	coast
coto privado de caza	private hunting area
Cruz Roja	Red Cross (medical aid)

cuesta	slope
cueva	cave
cumbre	summit

d

degollado	pass
derecha	right (direction)
desprendimiento	landslide

e

embalse	reservoir
ermita	chapel
Espacio Naturaleza Protegido	protected area of natural beauty
estación de autobus/guagua	bus station

f

farmacia	chemist
faro	lighthouse
fiesta	holiday, celebration
finca	farm, country house
fuente	spring

g

gasolinera	petrol station
guagua	bus
Guardia Civil	police
guia	guide

h

| hostal | hostel, accommodation |
| hoya | depression (geological) |

i

iglesia	church
información	information
isla	island
izquierda	left (direction)

l

lago	lake
lavadero	laundry area (usually communal)
librería	bookshop
llano	plain
lluvioso	rainy
lomo	broad-backed ridge

m

malpais	'bad lands' wild, barren countryside
mapa	map
mercado	market
mirador	lookout/viewing point
montaña	mountain

n

| nublado | cloudy |

o

oficina de turismo	tourist office

p

parapente	hang-glider
peligroso	dangerous
pensión	guesthouse
pico	peak
pista	dirt road/track
pista forestal	forest road/track
playa	beach
plaza	square
policia	police
pozo	well
prohibido el paso	no entry
puente	bridge
puerto	port, mountain pass

r

rambla	dry watercourse or riverbed
refugio	refuge, shelter
río	river, stream
roque	rock
ruta	route

s

salida	exit
senda	path, track
sendero	foot path
sierra	mountain range
sin salida	no through road/route

t

tajo	cliff, escarpment
tapas	bar snacks
tienda	shop
tipico	traditional bar/eating place
tormentoso	stormy
torre	tower
torrente	stream
tubería	water pipe

v

valle	valley
vega	meadow
ventoso	windy
vereda	path, lane
vivero	plant nursery, aboretum
volcán	volcano

z

zona recreativa	recreation area

RESEARCHING NEW WALKING ROUTES - A SIMPLE 'HOW-TO' GUIDE

Walkers who have used our guides and maps sometimes send us details of routes they've followed or discovered that aren't covered in our publications. Sometimes we are able to pass on their information to others, provided they send us sufficient detail.

If you are thinking of producing a walking route for other walkers, please read through our DWG guidelines for that research:

Maps
Does a map already show the details making up your walking route? In the UK, you're probably using OS maps which have all the walking trails, tracks (driveable), and tarmac roads, that you'll be following. If those details are already on an OS map then describing your route will be straightforward.

Recording information along the route
We use digital voice recorders for our notes as we walk a route. This is quicker and easier than making written notes. After completing the route we can then review the voice records to make a written description of the route.

Photos
Carry a digital camera so that you can take pictures of everything you think might be relevant. Your first picture should show the start point of your route. Features identifying locations along your route are much more useful than 'views' from the route. Especially useful are photos showing decision points along the walk. A phone can be used for your pictures but the quality may be marginal if you are publishing your route in printed form.

GPS
GPS is a great help in defining your walking route, especially if details of the route are not already shown on an official map, our usual DWG situation. Simply set your GPS track record to 'Auto' and record everything that you think might be useful as a waypoint; 'Mark' and 'Enter' on most GPS units.

Compass Directions
Compass directions can be really useful. While we are GPS users, we recognise the value of giving compass directions, confirmed on a hand held compass.

Walk at a Reasonable Pace
Walking routes should be an enjoyable adventure, not a race against time. Most of us walk at between 3 and 5kmh.

Record your times along your route
Most walkers have a watch or a phone telling them the time. Few, except GPS users, have anything that tells them the distance, so it makes sense to talk about the times taken along your route.

Use the information you've gathered to build your walk description. Make sure that you include all the key decision points where we need to make a choice about which trail/direction to take. It is easier to filter out unnecessary information after your research and walk description is complete. If you find you are short of key information, you may need to go back and re-walk your route!

Below is an example of a circular route on the island of Lanzarote, that James and Jan sent in to us at Discovery Walking Guides. They made clear notes as they walked the route they found, so that we were able to plot their route onto our Lanzarote Tour & Trail Map. Although James and Jan didn't use a GPS, the detail in their notes made it relatively easy to show their route clearly for others to follow. They did refer frequently to compass directions at decision points on the walk, and noted landmarks and natural features to keep walkers on the right route.

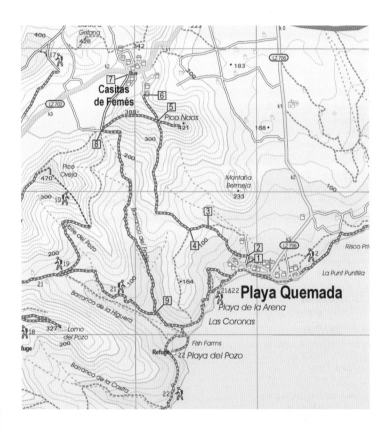

139

Send to: David & Ros at **ask.discovery@ntlworld.com**

Send to: David & Ros at **ask.discovery@ntlworld.com**